Hybrid Workflows in Translation

This concise volume serves as a valuable resource on understanding the integration and impact of generative AI (GenAI) and evolving technologies on translation workflows. As translation technologies continue to evolve rapidly, translation scholars and practicing translators need to address the challenges of how best to factor AI-enhanced tools into their practices and in translator training programmes.

The book covers a range of AI applications, including AI-powered features within Translation Management Systems, AI-based machine translation, AI-assisted translation, language generation modules and language checking tools. The volume puts the focus on using AI in translation responsibly and effectively, but also on ways to support students and practitioners in their professional development through easing technological anxieties and building digital resilience.

This book will be of interest to students, scholars and practitioners in translation and interpreting studies, as well as key stakeholders in the language services industry.

Michał Kornacki is Assistant Professor at the Institute of English Studies at the University of Łódź, Poland.

Paulina Pietrzak is Associate Professor at the Institute of English Studies at the University of Łódź, Poland.

Routledge Focus on Translation and Interpreting Studies

Translation and Social Media Communication in the Age of the Pandemic
Edited by Tong King Lee and Dingkun Wang

Translating Borrowed Tongues
The Verbal Quest of Ilan Stavans
Mª Carmen África Vidal Claramonte

Hybrid Workflows in Translation
Integrating GenAI into Translator Training
Michał Kornacki and Paulina Pietrzak

For more information about this series, please visit: www.routledge.com/Routledge-Focus-on-Translation-and-Interpreting-Studies/book-series/RFTIS

Hybrid Workflows in Translation

Integrating GenAI into Translator Training

Michał Kornacki and
Paulina Pietrzak

Taylor & Francis Group
NEW YORK AND LONDON

First published 2025
by Routledge
605 Third Avenue, New York, NY 10158

and by Routledge
4 Park Square, Milton Park, Abingdon, Oxon, OX14 4RN

Routledge is an imprint of the Taylor & Francis Group, an informa business

© 2025 Michał Kornacki and Paulina Pietrzak

The right of Michał Kornacki and Paulina Pietrzak to be identified as authors of this work has been asserted in accordance with sections 77 and 78 of the Copyright, Designs and Patents Act 1988.

All rights reserved. No part of this book may be reprinted or reproduced or utilised in any form or by any electronic, mechanical, or other means, now known or hereafter invented, including photocopying and recording, or in any information storage or retrieval system, without permission in writing from the publishers.

Trademark notice: Product or corporate names may be trademarks or registered trademarks, and are used only for identification and explanation without intent to infringe.

Library of Congress Cataloging-in-Publication Data
Names: Kornacki, Michał, 1982– author. | Pietrzak, Paulina, 1984– author.
Title: Hybrid workflows in translation : integrating GenAI into translator training / Michał Kornacki and Paulina Pietrzak.
Description: New York, NY : Routledge, 2025. |
Series: Routledge focus on translation and interpreting studies |
Includes bibliographical references and index.
Identifiers: LCCN 2024025849 | ISBN 9781032860473 (hardback) |
ISBN 9781032862095 (paperback) | ISBN 9781003521822 (ebook)
Subjects: LCSH: Translating and interpreting–Technological innovations. | Artificial intelligence. | Translators–Training of. | Translators–Attitudes.
Classification: LCC P306.97.T73 K67 2025 |
DDC 418/.02028563–dc23/eng/20240712
LC record available at https://lccn.loc.gov/2024025849

ISBN: 978-1-032-86047-3 (hbk)
ISBN: 978-1-032-86209-5 (pbk)
ISBN: 978-1-003-52182-2 (ebk)

DOI: 10.4324/9781003521822

Typeset in Times New Roman
by Newgen Publishing UK

Contents

List of figures   *vii*
List of tables   *viii*

Introduction   1
Overview of the book 1

1 (R)evolution of translation technology   6
   1.1 History and evolution of translation tools 6
      1.1.1 Machine translation 6
      1.1.2 Computer-assisted translation (CAT) tools 10
      1.1.3 Translation management systems 13
      1.1.4 Writing assistants and checking tools 14
      1.1.5 Generative artificial intelligence in translation 16
   1.2 The current state of translation technology 17
   1.3 Stages of AI development 18

2 Translator–AI interaction   30
   2.1 Augmented translation 30
   2.2 Hybrid workflows in translation 35
   2.3 The impact of technology on translator profession: new avenues and new anxieties 39
   2.4 Ethical considerations in AI-assisted language service provision 43

3 Translators as AI-assisted language specialists   51
   3.1 Translators' new roles and status 51

3.2 Future translator expertise: what is missing? 53
3.3 Technical skills for hybrid workflows 55
3.4 From anxiety to digital resilience 60
3.5 Personal resources and metacognitive capacity 64
3.6 The translator's self-concept in AI interactions 66

4 Attitudes towards AI in translation: an academic exploration 78
   4.1 Research design 78
   4.2 Limitations of the study 79
   4.3 Data analysis 81
      4.3.1 Findings on the use of AI technologies in translation 82
      4.3.2 Perspectives on GenAI integration in translator education 91
      4.3.3 Risks associated with using GenAI tools in translator training 94
   4.4 Summary of the findings: challenges and lessons learned 107

5 Implications for translator training 117
   5.1 To teach or not to teach? 117
   5.2 What's in it for translation students? 120
   5.3 Suggested ways of introducing AI-assisted translation practice 123
      5.3.1 Exercises in AI-assisted translation 123
      5.3.2 AI tools for terminology management 124
      5.3.3 AI-assisted quality assessment 126
      5.3.4 AI-generated feedback 127
      5.3.5 Ethical code of conduct in AI use 129
   5.4 Fostering personal resources in translator training 131
      5.4.1 Self-reflection: what am I missing? 131
      5.4.2 Self-efficacy: building digital resilience 134
      5.4.3 Self-concept: reducing technological anxiety 135

6 Final reflections 142

Appendix 144
   Attitudes toward AI in translation: an academic exploration 144
   Index 147

Figures

1.1	Estimated range for technology to achieve human-level performance, by technical capability	23
1.2	Median human-level AI estimate, (Roser, 2023), based on surveys conducted in 2018, 2019 and 2022	23
2.1	Augmented translation ties humans and machines together	33
4.1	Relationship map	86
4.2	Perceived benefits of GenAI (e.g. ChatGPT) for translation (total and by age and role)	88
4.3	Perceived impact of GenAI on the translation market (shown in percentage)	89
4.4	Impact of GenAI on the translation market: perspectives by role/profession and age (shown in percentage)	90
4.5	Impact of GenAI on translation and translation market (shown in percentage)	91
4.6	Perspectives on the integration of GenAI tools into translator training programmes (shown in percentage)	92
4.7	Responses on the extent to which GenAI tools (e.g. ChatGPT) should be used in translator training	94
4.8	Opinions on whether translation educators should be trained in using GenAI for pedagogical purposes (shown in percentage)	96
4.9	A comprehensive overview of the responses to questions about potential dangers	98

Tables

1.1	Comparison of ANI, AGI and ASI	22
4.1	Demographic structure of the sample (n = 151)	82
4.2	AI-powered tools used in translation (total and by role/profession)	84
4.3	AI-powered tools used in translation (total and by age)	85
4.4	Number of tools in use by role/profession and age	87
4.5	Levels of agreement on GenAI tools integration into translator training programmes (by role/profession and age)	93
4.6	Opinions on the extent to which GenAI tools (e.g. ChatGPT) should be used in translator training (by role/profession and age)	95
4.7	Opinions on whether translation educators should be trained in using GenAI for pedagogical purposes (by role/profession and age)	97
4.8	Risks associated with the use of GenAI tools in translator training (total and by role/profession)	100
4.9	Risks associated with the use of GenAI tools in translator training (total and by age)	102
4.10	Correlation analysis of perceptions regarding GenAI's benefits, market impact, usage versus risk evaluation	104
4.11	Usage of AI tools and opinions on the potential risks associated with using GenAI tools in translator training (means comparison)	105
4.12	Hierarchy of risks associated with using GenAI tools in translator training correlated with AI technologies used by respondents	106

Introduction

Overview of the book

This book examines the evolving interaction between human translators and AI technologies, specifically focusing on the integration of technology into translation workflows and the balance between automation and translator expertise. The scope includes an analysis of the current state of translation technology, an exploration of AI-enhanced tools and the challenges of incorporating them into translator training programs. Intending to contribute to discussions on the responsible and effective use of AI in translation, the book advocates for a collaborative approach that combines the unique resources of human translators with the capabilities of AI tools.

The book reports on an exploratory study on perceptions and expectations of translation practitioners, translator educators and translation trainees, providing insights into the mindset surrounding AI technologies. The data collected and analysed using statistical quantitative correlational methods reflect the attitudes towards GenAI and unravel the ethical and professional considerations associated with the integration. The findings show that a large group of translators are not optimistic about the recent advancements, with almost half of the respondents not seeing any benefits from GenAI. The findings show a number of reasons why they are sceptical regarding the impact of GenAI on the translation market, but what differentiates opinions in this regard is the respondent's role or profession. The data show that respondent groups display varying degrees of enthusiasm towards introducing AI into translator training.

While providing insights and recommendations, the book does not claim to offer exhaustive solutions to the challenges of AI integration

DOI: 10.4324/9781003521822-1

in translation or translator training, but proposes a framework for fostering a collaborative interaction between the unique abilities of human translators and the aid offered by AI tools. The book asserts that a synergistic relationship between human translators and AI technologies has the potential to significantly enhance translation quality and efficiency; this improvement, however, is dependent on thorough ethical considerations and the thoughtful fostering of translators' personal resources such as self-efficacy, self-regulation or self-concept. This approach emphasises the critical role of technical skills but also metacognitive capacity enhancement within translator training programs, aiming to prepare future translators for the challenges and opportunities presented by a digitised, AI-enhanced professional environment.

Despite their rapid evolution and modification, one of the constant aspects of translation technologies is that "they are not merely supplementary tools but, in fact, actively modify the very essence of the cognitive activity undertaken by translators" (cf. Pym 2011: 1). Given the recent technological advancements that can enhance productivity and efficiency to unprecedented levels, it becomes essential to recognise the emerging challenges that significantly impact translators' workflows, necessitating a thoughtful approach to their integration and application. Artificial intelligence (AI) technologies are not just aids but they actively alter the fundamental nature of cognitive activities performed by translators. As the technologies employed in translation grow more complex, the interaction between these tools and the translation process, as well as with translators themselves, becomes increasingly intricate and transformative.

In the study on the usage of computer-assisted translation (CAT) tools in translator training (2021), the authors observed a noticeable presence of a sense of unease, worry and apprehension specifically pertaining to technology among freelance translators. It seems imperative now to examine even more powerful AI technologies, exploring their impact on the translation market, particularly on translators and educators and determining the necessary steps to integrate them reasonably into translator training. The primary goal of this book is to investigate the integration of generative AI (GenAI) into translation processes. This research is grounded in the evolving landscape of translation technology, prompted by advancements in AI that challenge traditional practices. The discussion, centring particularly on GenAI, spans a range of AI applications, including AI-powered features within Translation Management Systems (TMS), AI-based machine translation, AI-assisted translation, language generation modules and language checking tools. The book discusses the concept of augmented translation and new hybrid workflows in today's translation industry. It explores new roles and status of translators as AI-assisted language specialists, examining the competencies that may be lacking as new technologies emerge. It addresses widespread concerns resulting from the impact of automation on the translation sector, exploring how translators can foster better digital resilience. It touches upon the translator's metacognitive capacity and the psychological capital in the face of translator-AI interactions and considers how translators' self-concept and the capacity for adaptability can support their professional evolution in a rapidly transforming industry. The findings of a survey regarding attitudes towards GenAI unravel the ethical and professional considerations associated with the integration, contributing to discussions on responsible and effective use of AI in translation. The survey captures the perceptions and expectations of translation practitioners, translator educators and translation trainees, providing insights into the mindset surrounding AI technologies.

Given that translators and other language service providers must adapt to innovations and new workflows, translation trainees may also need to engage with AI technologies to ensure their relevance and competitiveness in the constantly evolving language services industry. Special attention, however, should be devoted to fostering translation students' personal growth alongside technical proficiency. The book explores methods for achieving a balance between human potential and technological efficiency in translation education with a particular focus on the importance of enhancing metacognitive skills as a means to reinforce digital resilience and mitigate technological anxieties. Through this approach, the study aims to contribute to a more balanced and productive educational framework.

The book begins with an examination of the current state of translation technology in Chapter 1. To appreciate the current state of translation technology, it is crucial to begin with tracing its historical evolution. This chapter includes an exploration of the historical development of translation tools, machine translation, translation memory systems and the role of natural language processing and GenAI in the translation process. It provides an overview of how these technologies have evolved and their current state in the field. The chapter also explores the stages of AI development, underscoring its present state and anticipated future advancements.

In the second chapter, the book specifically examines the complex relationship between human translators and AI, highlighting how AI influences translation workflows, quality and the profession as a whole. This chapter delves into concepts like augmented translation within hybrid workflows, describing and exemplifying the collaborative interaction between translators and GenAI systems. It provides an analysis of the interaction between translators and AI systems, highlighting how this collaboration can optimise translation processes and outcomes. This chapter explores the dual aspects of opportunities and challenges arising from GenAI integration in translation, highlighting the transformative potential and the accompanying ethical, professional and educational considerations. Lastly, the chapter also examines the ethical implications and potential ways of ensuring that translators can adapt to and thrive in a landscape transformed by AI.

Chapter 3 discusses the status of the translator as AI-assisted language specialist. It looks at future translator competences and the necessary skillset that translators must acquire in this changing environment, which is not limited to technical or instrumental competences, but includes the psychological capital of the translator which can have an impact on how successful they are in pursuing a career in language industry. The chapter investigates the concerns and technological anxiety among translators regarding job insecurity and the challenges posed by automation in the translation industry. It explores the translator's metacognitive capacity and looks into the translator's self-concept with the underlying factors that allow for adaptability and self-development in rapidly changing translation industry.

Next, Chapter 4 covers the methodological framework of the study into the attitudes and insights of translation professionals, academics and students regarding the incorporation of GenAI in translator education. The chapter discusses the results of the study conducted to explore the diverse attitudes towards AI, assessing how these views vary among different stakeholders in the field. The research was carried out from late 2023 to early 2024 employing the computer-assisted web interview (CAWI) methodology in order to administer a survey to the targeted population comprising translators, translator educators and translation trainees. The resulting data, reviewed and analysed with SPSS statistics software using quantitative correlational methods, captures the attitudes to AI, that is, the use of various AI-powered tools, the need for introducing GenAI into translator education, as well as the implications of using GenAI in translator training. The chapter covers the methodological framework of the study and presents the findings with statistical analysis and discussion. It also presents final reflections and lessons learned from this exploration, highlighting significant trends and opinions.

Chapter 5 discusses whether GenAI should be a part of translator training and analyses the challenges and potential impacts of this integration on the future of the translation profession. The chapter addresses the complexities of integrating GenAI with human expertise in translator training, examining the role and function of AI in educational settings. The chapter concludes by presenting a selection of methods for incorporating AI in translation education and exemplary ways of fostering personal resources of translation students, helping them reduce technological anxieties and build digital resilience. Central to the discussion is the emphasis on the role of technology as a complement to, rather than a replacement for, human expertise.

The concluding reflections in Chapter 6 emphasise the notion that adaptation and metacognitive skill enhancement are fundamental, highlighting the dynamic evolution of the translator's role within hybrid translation workflows so heavily influenced by automation. With particular attention to encouraging responsible educational practices aligned with the demands of modern language services, the approach presented here is intended to foster an educational framework that equips future translators with the skills and knowledge to thrive in a digitised, AI-driven world.

Reference

Pym, Anthony. 2011. 'What Technology Does to Translating'. *International Journal for Translation & Interpreting Research* 3 (1): 1–9.

1 (R)evolution of translation technology

1.1 History and evolution of translation tools

The topic of the history of translation is quite vast and significant for the current exploration. It can be traced back to around 2150 to 2000 BCE when "The Epic of Gilgamesh", a Sumerian poem, was written in Sumerian cuneiform script and later translated into Akkadian (George, 2003). The discussion then moves to the ancient forums of Greece and Rome, the monasteries of Spain, France and England during the Middle Ages, and the dining halls of Renaissance and Modernity. However, the emphasis of this analysis is on technological advancements that led to the development of translation technology and the ideas that contributed to the evolution of translation practices, rather than providing an overview of translation's historical development. For a more comprehensive account, please refer to such publications as Kelly (1995), Windle and Pym (2011) or Long (2007), among others.

1.1.1 Machine translation

Translation technology, as the authors understand it today, includes such tools or services as machine translation (MT), computer-assisted translation (CAT), translation management systems (TMS), writing assistants and checking tools, as well as GenAI, to name just the main categories. Their evolution is interconnected, to a degree. Arguably, the first tool, or technology, to be discussed in the book is machine translation.

While MT is dependent on technology (computing, in particular) and, therefore, could not develop before computers were invented, its

DOI: 10.4324/9781003521822-2

founding principles had been formed much earlier. We can trace the first proto-MT ideas to Descartes (1596–1650) who believed mathematics and mechanics could explain the processes taking place in the human mind, which he compared to a machine. His ideas extended to language as well. He formulated an idea that a dictionary printed in all the languages could help to "mechanise" the process of translation, which can be seen "as a prefiguration of how an interlingual 'mechanical' dictionary might work" (Hutchins 1997: online). His idea was followed up by Becher's complex yet groundbreaking ideas for machine translation, including attaching glossaries to a universal language, which were revisited and published in the 1960s as an example of pre-computer instructions (or program) for machine translation (Becher, 1962).

However, if the 17th-century ideas for MT are to be disregarded, the actual beginning of MT dates to the 1930s when Russian scholar Petr Troyanskii introduced foundational ideas emphasising human-assisted MT, where translation is machine-performed but requires human pre- and post-processing (Hutchins, 2010: 434). Conversely, Warren Weaver and Andrew Booth were among the first to suggest using newly invented computers for translating natural languages, independent of extensive human intervention (Chan 2004: 290–291). In 1949, Weaver published a memorandum, suggesting the application of cryptography, statistical methods, Claude Shannon's information theory and exploiting the logical features of languages (Kornacki, 2018) in machine translation. The reception of the memorandum was varied, however. Many scholars believed any language to be too complex to be successfully processed by a machine. At the same time, researchers like Erwin Reifler found the idea promising. Reifler suggested how simple word-for-word translations can be used in a system involving text pre- and post-editing (idem).

In the 1950s, the development of MT gained momentum. The Massachusetts Institute of Technology (MIT) held the first conference on MT in 1952, which introduced several new ideas regarding pre- and post-editing, appropriate target lexical items selection and a sort of syntactic structure analysis. However, the most significant conclusion was that a public demonstration of a functional MT system was necessary to attract funding. The presentation occurred in 1954 at Georgetown, where an MT system was used to translate a pre-selected sample from Russian to English. The presentation attracted much attention, resulting in substantial funding for the project in the

US. However, the global interest in MT was even more impressive (Kornacki, 2018).

Over the following decade, more and more problems started to appear. Some of them resulted from the fact that no appropriate technology was available yet. Others related to purely linguistic problems. Several prominent individuals (e.g. Bar-Hillel, see Green, Heer & Manning, 2015) claimed that the very principles of MT were flawed. The popular belief at the time was that the goal of MT was to create a system that could produce a human-quality level of translation without human intervention (fully automated high-quality translation [FAHQT]). The problem was, as the ongoing research suggested, that the idea was not only limited by the technology – it was theoretically impossible to achieve. A solution might have been found if the problem was to remain in an academic domain. However, many parties invested money and needed to see if the investment would pay back. Therefore, the US government set up the Automatic Language Processing Advisory Committee (ALPAC) in order to examine the situation. The 1966 ALPAC report said that "MT was slower, less accurate and twice as expensive as human translation and that there is no immediate or predictable prospect of useful machine translation" (Hutchins 1995, online). Moreover, the report recommended the development of machine aids for translators and the continued support of basic research in computational linguistics. MT turned out to be costly, time-consuming (the need for pre- and post-editing) and of low quality. Therefore, by suggesting the development of other-than-MT computer-based aids for translators, the report marked the end of the research on MT in the US.

The research on MT entered a period of stagnation. This is not to say that there were no breakthroughs. Canada required reliable translation services to support its bicultural policy while Europe had to deal with the growing need for translation within the European Community. This led to the creation of Météo, which was employed to translate Canadian weather forecasts since 1976. Other important systems included (see Hutchins 2010):

- French TITUS
- Chinese CULT
- Japanese ATLAS
- SYSTRAN
- Xerox Corporation MT and
- MT system developed by the Logos Corporation

The success of the abovementioned systems reignited the spark of interest in MT. Advancements in the development of computers, as well as the new research in computational linguistics, significantly contributed to restarting the interest in MT in the 1980s. First and foremost, researchers and translation service providers realised that a change in the approach to MT was required. They did not need a system that could provide FAHQT services, but rather a tool that would aid human translators in the translation process. Kornacki (2018: 100) mentions that the "role of MT changed from a utopian system meant to replace human translator to a component of translator's workshop". While it is still successfully employed in domain-restricted systems for specific purposes (Xerox, Microsoft) and as a service for non-translators (auto-translation of web pages, free online MT systems like Google Translate or DeepL) (Hutchins, 1995, 2006), the authors believe that it is critical to consider MT as an aid for a professional translator, not a replacement for his/her services.

The period of "revival" of the interest in MT, which can be considered to have lasted from the 1980s to 2010s, saw a growing progress in the quality of MT output. The initial MT systems were rule-based, which was actually one of the very first MT strategies to be developed. "More complex than translating word to word, these systems develop[ed] linguistic rules that allow[ed] words to be put in different places, to have different meanings depending on context, etc." (Costa-Jussà et al., 2012: 248). Rule-based MT (RBMT) offered consistent and predictable quality at the cost of complexity and being expensive. RBMT is based on rules (grammatical, lexical and stylistic), the application of numerous bilingual dictionaries for each language pair and software able to handle the data to produce a successful translation. The drawback of such an approach to MT was that for the system to provide acceptable translation, a lot of linguistic resources and time was required. What it means is that an RBMT system is expensive to build, and it can be even more costly to customise.

Statistical machine translation (SMT) takes on a different approach. It utilises multilingual corpora to identify statistical patterns and rules, which can be later used in the process of translation (Koehn 2009). Its performance is directly related to the number and quality of the corpora available for the system. Instead of words, SMT systems use phrases as basic units of translation and produce translations "using the overlap in phrases" (Costa-Jussà et al., 2012: 249). However, their very nature and dependence on raw data that required to be processed in real-time meant that an average SMT system depended on the computing power of contemporary computers, which was not significant (compared to modern computers) and acted as a solid limiter to their wider use.

Hybrid MT systems combine the best features of different types of machine translation methodologies, such as rule-based machine translation (RBMT), statistical machine translation (SMT) and neural machine translation (NMT), to leverage the strengths and mitigate the weaknesses of each individual approach. This combination can address specific challenges like handling idiomatic expressions, maintaining consistency and ensuring fluency. Hybrid systems can be more adaptable to various types of texts and languages, including those with limited available data or complex grammatical structures. The synergy of different methods often results in translations that are more accurate and maintain the context and stylistic nuances better than systems relying on a single approach. Examples of hybrid systems include Google Translate (in its previous iterations) which involved both RBMT for basic grammatical structures and SMT for handling large-scale bilingual corpora before fully transitioning to NMT, or SYSTRAN which has been developed to combine rule-based and statistical translation methods, aiming to provide more accurate translations, especially for languages with less digital data (idem.).

The introduction of the abovementioned neural machine translation marked the neural revolution in the mid-2010s. NMT systems use deep learning, particularly sequence-to-sequence models like recurrent neural networks (RNNs) and later transformers, to provide more contextually aware and fluent translations. Today, NMT systems continue to evolve, integrating more advanced neural network architectures and addressing challenges such as handling low-resource languages and domain-specific translations. Recent advancements in the development of AI and its integration with NMT systems continue to push the boundaries of what is possible in MT. While MT in itself is very helpful, it is most commonly used by translators within a translation environment called computer-assisted translation (CAT) tools, discussed in the next section.

1.1.2 Computer-assisted translation (CAT) tools

CAT tools came to be in the first place due to the perceived failure of early MT systems. Kornacki (2018) mentions that the publication of the ALPAC report and the subsequent redirection of research in the field of machine translation (MT) enabled scholars to move away from the overly optimistic presuppositions initially associated with MT and to instead concentrate on developing both linguistic and computational strategies that could enhance machine translation capabilities. This shift was instrumental in fostering corpus-based and statistical methodologies research, which ultimately established the groundwork for computer-assisted translation.

The advent of corpus-based frameworks, alongside novel data storage and retrieval methods, facilitated the establishment of foundational principles for translation memory (TM) systems (Bowker & Fisher, 2010). TM systems, which are essentially bilingual corpora, provide the capability to retrieve and utilise past translations in ongoing projects (Zanettin, 2012). Despite the utility of TM as a standalone resource, translators expressed a need for more versatile tools that could streamline the translation process (Austermühl, 2001). Recognising this demand, the market responded with the introduction of the first CAT tools. The initial foray into this technology was the Translation Support System (TSS), developed by Automated Language Processing Systems (ALPS) in the mid-1980s (Somers, 2003). However, the market at that time was not technologically prepared for the widespread adoption of such tools, as many translators were still reliant on typewriters (Olohan, 2015). The transition from typewriters to home personal computers (PCs) equipped with word processors – and eventually connected to the internet – marked a significant technological shift. By the mid-1990s, the affordability and versatility of PCs had increased to the point where acquiring one was no longer a significant financial investment (Chan, 2015).

This technological evolution set the stage for introducing new CAT tools into the market. Various tools emerged, including Trados, Translator's Workbench, MultiTerm (a terminology database), Translation Manager 2, Transit, Déjà Vu and the now-discontinued Eurolang Optimiser. The efficacy of these tools varied, but it was Trados that, "thanks to successful European Commission tender bids in 1996 and 1997 – that found itself the tool of choice of the main players, and, thus, the default industry standard" (Garcia 2015: 70). The competitive landscape was intense, compelling the early CAT tools to undergo significant evolution. By the late 1990s, more sophisticated systems offered features such as translation memory, alignment tools, terminology management and a variety of file-processing filters (Bowker,

2002). CAT tools have been designed to aid translators in their work, enhancing both the efficiency and quality of translations. The key ideas behind their creation and use were (and still are):

- increased efficiency
- consistency in translation
- quality improvement
- resource management
- collaboration facilitation
- integration with other tools
- cost reduction

Recent advancements in CAT tools have focused on refining existing features and incorporating innovative technologies such as MT and AI. MT remains one of the central components in the CAT environment, now integrated as a module in most contemporary CAT tools, which allows the integration of multiple commercial MT plugins. AI integration is visible in features like, for example, Phrase Language AI developed by Phrase for their home TMS system, which uses AI features to determine "the optimal MT engine for translation jobs, based on each job's domain and language pair" (Phrase TMS, 2024: online). However, CAT software developers go even further than MT evaluation. Trados is about to launch (at the time this book is written) its own LLM which will help translators in several ways. Pooley (2023: online) hints that translators will be able to send to the LLM the following information:

- "How other segments in the same document have been translated;
- How similar segments were translated in the past (re-using fuzzy match technology);
- Which terms have been identified in the source text and how they should be translated;
- The required style of translation (formal, informal, friendly, professional etc.);
- Other settings like maximum length or gender-neutral language."

All this data will allow the LLM to improve its generative output and provide the translator with better suggestions. However, details of what happens with the submitted data are still unclear. Trados claims their private LLM can be trained with the user data, which suggests data pooling for, supposedly, mutual benefit – and data pooling is something translators do not like due to data confidentiality policies they are part of. The exact nature of the proposed solution is yet to be seen, but the idea is promising and something to be considered by other CAT developers.

In summary, the field of computer-assisted translation has evolved considerably since the 1966 ALPAC report's critical assessment of MT. The redefined role of MT has facilitated the advancement of CAT tools and enhanced MT itself, now purposed to complement human translators' expertise rather than supplant it. Although the future direction of CAT tools is yet to be fully determined (namely due to the implementation of NMT systems and the emergence of large language model (LLM)-based AI), current trends do indicate the need for further improvement, if not a redefinition of the basic concept of CAT tools as such.

1.1.3 Translation management systems

Translation management systems (TMS) represent a pivotal aspect in the evolving landscape of language translation, offering an integrated approach to managing the complex process of translating documents across various languages. Embodying a fusion of technology and linguistics, these systems streamline the translation workflow, thereby enhancing efficiency and accuracy (see Austermühl, 2001; Jiménez-Crespo, 2013; Kornacki, 2018).

At first glance, it may be unclear how TMS are different from CAT tools. The explanation lies in the scope of both notions. At the core of most state-of-the-art TMS is a software solution designed to facilitate and automate the translation process. It serves as a central hub for all translation-related activities, including project management, workflow automation, collaboration and integration of translation memories and glossaries (Jiménez-Crespo, 2013). Basically, it is a CAT tool. However, where a CAT tool offers basic features in terms of project management, collaboration and integration, a TMS provides a centralised system for handling multiple translation projects, tracking progress and managing resources. TMS allow project managers to assign tasks, track deadlines and oversee multiple projects simultaneously. They can automate workflow steps, from the initial quote to final delivery, and can integrate with client systems for seamless project transitions (Kenny, 2011; Herbert et al. 2023). What is more, they often feature robust collaboration tools, allowing multiple translators, editors and project managers to work together effectively. Some of the most known TMS on the market are SDL Trados Studio, memoQ, Phrase, XTRF and GlobalLink, to name just a few.

TMS increasingly use AI in areas like automated workflow management (e.g., AI can automate several aspects of the translation workflow, such as project assignment, deadline estimations and resource allocation based on the complexity of the text, translator expertise and past performance data); predictive analysis (e.g., AI can analyse historical data to provide insights and predictions on project timelines, costs and resource requirements. This helps in better planning and managing translation projects); and client interaction and support (e.g., AI-powered chatbots and virtual assistants can be integrated into TMS to provide support for clients in areas like: automated quotes; document submission, technical assistance in terms of TMS integration in the client's system, and more). To sum it up, TMS are mainly used by translation agencies and large organisations that handle a high volume of translation work and require comprehensive management of these processes. On the other hand, CAT tools are primarily used by individual translators or small teams focusing on the translation task itself. They are essential for translators aiming to enhance their productivity and maintain quality.

1.1.4 Writing assistants and checking tools

Writing assistants, such as Grammarly, DeepL Write or Microsoft Editor, represent a significant evolution in the domain of language processing and translation, marking a pivotal shift in how text is composed, analysed and refined. These tools, underpinned by advanced artificial intelligence (AI) algorithms, serve to augment the writing process, offering nuanced and context-aware suggestions that go beyond mere spellchecking (see Frankenberg-Garcia et al., 2019; Pokrivcakova, 2019). At least, such is the theory. In practice, avid users will see that the suggestions of changes offered by those tools are not always 100% accurate or they change the idea that the writer wanted to convey. While this may deter many individuals, it has to be remembered that, as with any AI-powered writing tool, human interaction (proofreading or post-processing) is fundamental – tools are there to facilitate our work, not do it for us (Gayed et al., 2022). What is more, it needs to be noted that in some cases (e.g. Grammarly) the efficiency and the number of features of the tool increases when the paid version is used.

The genesis of writing assistants can be traced back to the early days of computer-assisted writing tools, which primarily focused on basic grammar and spellcheck functions. However, AI and machine learning technologies (Brynjolfsson and McAfee, 2014) have revolutionised these tools. Modern writing assistants leverage sophisticated algorithms to understand the grammatical correctness and the context, tone and style of the written text. This evolution is deeply rooted in the advancements in natural language processing (NLP) and machine learning, fields that have seen exponential growth in recent years (Godwin-Jones, 2022).

AI plays a central role in the operation of these tools. By employing techniques such as deep learning, a subset of machine learning, writing assistants can analyse vast amounts of text and learn from the nuances of language usage. This enables them to provide contextually appropriate and stylistically consistent suggestions, thereby enhancing the written content's overall quality.

The primary aim of writing assistants is to aid users in producing clear, effective, and error-free text. They serve as a virtual aide, ensuring linguistic accuracy and stylistic appropriateness. For professional translators, these tools offer invaluable assistance in several ways. In regular translation workflows, writing assistants can help in ensuring the grammatical integrity and readability of translated text. They can serve as a final check to ensure that the translation is accurate and reads naturally in the target language.

In the context of MT and CAT workflows, writing assistants can play a pivotal role in post-editing processes. Machine translation, while efficient, often lacks the nuanced understanding of language that a human translator possesses. Writing assistants can bridge this gap by identifying and suggesting corrections in areas where the machine translation may fall short, such as idiomatic expressions or subtle language nuances. While the same can be said about CAT-based translation, it must be mentioned that CAT tools segment text to allow human translators to translate it. Therefore, the resulting translation is primarily sentence for sentence, which may be detrimental to the final clarity of the text. Post-editing with writing assistants can help to identify and mitigate such problems, but to some extent only. In order to provide a level of correction that "sees" above the context of neighbouring sentences, other tools have to be used, primarily GenAI.

In conclusion, writing assistants represent a confluence of linguistics and AI, providing a sophisticated layer of language analysis that, if consciously used, enhance the translation process and reflect the dynamic interplay of human expertise and machine intelligence in the field of language translation.

1.1.5 Generative artificial intelligence in translation

The beginnings of GenAI in translation can be traced back to the early days of computational linguistics and machine translation. These initial steps, rooted in rule-based systems, laid the critical groundwork for AI's application in translation (Lopez, 2008; Koehn, 2009). In these formative years, the focus was on creating algorithms that could translate text based on a set of predefined grammatical and lexical rules. While these systems were foundational, they were limited by their inability to adapt to human languages' linguistic nuances and context variability.

Their evolution was closely bound with that of MT. A significant paradigm shift occurred with the transition to SMT. However, the most transformative moment in this evolutionary trajectory was the introduction of NMT (both SMT and NMT were discussed in section 2.1.1). NMT represented a leap forward in translation technology, employing deep learning and artificial neural networks to capture the contextual nuances of language. Unlike its predecessors, NMT does not rely on discrete phrases or words but rather considers the entire input sequence, enabling it to produce more fluent and accurate translations. The deep learning algorithms at the heart of NMT allow for processing vast amounts of data and learning complex patterns and intricacies of language in a way that mimics human cognition (Melby, 2019).

GenAI, on the other hand, refers to the broader set of AI technologies that can generate new content. This includes not just text, but also images, music, code, and more. In the context of translation, GenAI is seen in the development of models that can generate human-like, coherent, and contextually relevant text based on training from large language datasets. The most notable examples of GenAI in translation are the generative pre-trained transformers (GPTs) and similar models, which use deep learning techniques to produce text that mimics human writing styles and patterns (Cao et al., 2023).

The relationship between GenAI and NMT is thus one of extension and integration rather than replacement. GenAI models, particularly those based on transformer architectures, have been integrated into NMT systems to enhance their capabilities. These models contribute to the translation process by improving understanding of context, idiomatic expressions, and stylistic nuances. Additionally, GenAI can assist in tasks closely related to translation, such as paraphrasing, summarising and creating multilingual content that retains the original's tone and style.

In summary, while NMT represents a significant leap in translation technology, GenAI is an overarching technology that includes NMT as one of its applications. The integration of GenAI into NMT systems represents the evolution of translation technology, where the boundaries of machine translation are continually being expanded to achieve greater fluency, accuracy, and contextual relevance.

1.2 The current state of translation technology

The preceding section aimed to provide an overview of the significant developments in translation technology, focusing on aspects considered most crucial and explaining the application of these technological advancements in the field of translation. The following section aims to summarise the above and provide additional insights.

The current state of translation technology is a dynamic and evolving landscape, marked by significant advancements and challenges that are shaping the future of translation practices. In this detailed overview, we explore the technologies most commonly used by translators, the mastery and market expectations of translation technology, its current limitations, and the prospective impact on the future of translation.

Today's translation industry relies heavily on sophisticated technologies such as CAT tools, TM systems and NMT. CAT tools, including widely used platforms like SDL Trados and MemoQ, offer translators an integrated environment to streamline their workflow, enhanced by the capabilities of TM systems that store and reuse previously translated segments. NMT, a breakthrough in machine translation, employs deep learning algorithms to deliver translations with unprecedented fluency and contextual accuracy. The potential for further enhancement lies in the deeper integration of AI, which promises to extend the capabilities of these tools, especially in handling diverse linguistic structures and specialised domains (Baker & Saldanha, 2019; Camgoz et al., 2020; Kong, 2022; Pym, 2023).

In translation technology, a growing expectation exists for translators to be proficient with these advanced tools. Mastery of CAT tools, TM systems and NMT is increasingly seen as integral to professional translation, driven by market demands for efficiency, consistency and speed. This expectation underscores a shift in the translator's role, where technical expertise becomes as crucial as linguistic skills (Groves & Mundt, 2015; Pietrzak & Kornacki, 2021; Vieira 2020, Vieira et al., 2021).

Despite the advancements, translation technologies are not without limitations. Challenges such as handling low-resource languages and domain-specific terminologies often require human expertise. NMT, while sophisticated, frequently struggles with cultural nuances and idiomatic expressions, necessitating human intervention. These technological constraints necessitate a balanced approach, where translators must judiciously use technology while relying on their linguistic and cultural expertise (Bentivogli et al., 2020).

With its blend of AI-driven advancements and inherent challenges, the current trajectory of translation technology is paving the way for a future where translation is about converting text and facilitating seamless multilingual communication. Future developments are likely to focus on enhancing the capabilities of NMT, exploring new frontiers in AI, and finding innovative ways to integrate human expertise with machine efficiency. This evolving landscape suggests a future where translation technology transcends its current limitations, offering more nuanced and culturally sensitive translations (Cao et al., 2018; Jiang & Lu, 2021; Khurana et al., 2023).

The state of translation technology today is a testament to the remarkable progress in the field, intertwined with challenges that spur continuous innovation. As technology advances, it reshapes the practice of translation, setting the stage for a future that promises even greater integration of human and machine capabilities in overcoming language barriers. However, this discussion would not be complete without proper consideration of the current stage of development of AI and its capabilities.

1.3 Stages of AI development

The development stages of AI provide a useful framework for understanding how translation technologies have evolved over time. From rule-based systems to current NMT models, each stage represents a significant leap in the capabilities and accuracy of translation tools. By understanding these stages, translators can appreciate the technological advancements that have impacted their profession and anticipate future trends.

As AI continues to advance, the role of human translators is expected to change. The transition from Narrow AI to potential future stages, such as Artificial General Intelligence and Artificial Super Intelligence, could significantly alter the translation landscape. By understanding the trajectory of AI development, translators can better prepare for future challenges and opportunities, especially if they realise the current stage of AI development. This might include acquiring new skills or exploring niches where human translation remains irreplaceable. Awareness of AI development stages also encourages continuous learning and adaptation, which are essential for thriving in a rapidly changing profession.

With AI gaining a huge amount of attention from the general audience, it is possible to determine between three and ten stages of AI development. The broader classification, based on thoughts by people like Igor van Gemert (2023) – an IT specialist with a background in cybersecurity and AI, and rather popular in the internet media – includes:

1 **Rule or Knowledge-Based Systems** – early AI systems that operate on predefined rules and knowledge bases;
2 **Context-Based & Retention Systems** – these systems can understand the context and retain information over sessions;
3 **Narrow Domain or Expert AI Systems** – AI systems specialised in specific domains, excelling in specific tasks and replicating human expertise in fields like medicine, finance, gaming and language translation;
4 **Reasoning AI Systems** – AI systems designed to simulate human-like reasoning and decision-making processes using logical reasoning and inferences based on provided information;
5 **Self-Aware Systems** – AI that possesses self-awareness and consciousness that can introspect and develop an understanding of itself;
6 **Artificial General Intelligence** – AI that can learn, reason and perform a wide range of actions on a human level (see more below);
7 **Artificial Super Intelligence** – AI that surpasses human intelligence across all fields (see more below);

8 **Transcendent AI** – hypothetical AI that has evolved beyond current understanding and capability (Sarsia et al., 2023), potentially merging with advanced technologies to enhance or create new forms of intelligence;
9 **Cosmic AI** – hypothetical AI that operates at a cosmic scale, potentially involving intelligence that spans galaxies or the universe;
10 **God-Like AI** – hypothetical AI with omnipotent and omniscient capabilities.

Given that 40% of the above list remains hypothetical, a narrower list might be better to serve as a basis for future discussion. Mucci & Stryker (2023) suggest the following:

1 Narrow AI, also known as **Artificial Narrow Intelligence (ANI)** or Weak AI. ChatGPT, one of the most widely known public AIs, falls into the category. ANI refers to artificial intelligence systems designed to perform a narrow task (e.g., facial recognition or internet searches) without possessing consciousness, sentience, or general intelligence (Bundy, 2017; Jungherr, 2023; Mucci & Stryker, 2023). These systems are highly specialised and can outperform humans at their specific tasks due to their efficiency and ability to process large datasets quickly. At the moment, the publicly available AI tools suggest that the development of AI is at this particular stage.
2 **Artificial General Intelligence (AGI)**. AGI, which is also known as strong AI (Kurzweil, 2005; James, 2021), full AI (James, 2021), human-level AI (Roser, 2023) or general intelligent action (Newell and Simon, 1976), refers to a type of AI that can learn, reason and perform a diverse range of actions similar to humans. However, some academic sources reserve the term "strong AI" for computer programs that experience sentience or consciousness. The ultimate objective of developing AGI is to create machines that can execute multiple tasks and function as human-like, equally intelligent assistants in our day-to-day lives (Altman, 2023). Or, to put it in other words, it will be a machine that is "able to learn to do anything a human can do" (Russel & Norvig, 2021: 50).
3 **Artificial Superintelligence (ASI)**, or super AI, represents a theoretical form of artificial intelligence that surpasses human intelligence across all fields, including creativity, general wisdom and

problem-solving. ASI would not only be capable of mimicking human intelligence and capabilities but would significantly exceed them (Yampolskiy, 2015; Barrett & Baum, 2017; Baum et al., 2017), leading to innovations and decision-making at levels incomprehensible to humans. The concept of ASI raises both opportunities and risks, prompting discussions on ethical implications, control and governance (Altman et al., 2023). ASI would act as the backbone technology of a completely self-aware AI that can self-improve. The idea behind it is also the reason why the media often portrays the "AI takeover" as a recurring theme. But at this point, it's all speculation.

Below is a point-by-point comparison of ANI, AGI and ASI, highlighting their capabilities, scope and differences (see Goertzel & Pennachin, 2007; Bostrom, 2014; Bostrom & Yudkowski 2014; Yampolskiy, 2015; Brooks, 2017; James, 2021; Russel & Norvig, 2021).

The discussion highlights that we are still in the early stages of AI development, and that despite its current capabilities, AI has tremendous untapped potential. The figure below shows the estimated range for AI technology to achieve human-level performance, based on pre-generative (2017) and post-generative AI (2023) capabilities. It is evident that progress has been faster than expected in some areas.

Looking forward, the progression from the present stage towards AGI, and subsequently to ASI, represents a significant stride in technological advancement. It needs to be stressed that AGI remains a theoretical concept at this point. Achieving AGI would signify the creation of machines capable of executing multiple tasks and functioning as human-like, equally intelligent assistants in our daily lives. This transition would mark a pivotal point in AI development, potentially reshaping various aspects of the world, including employment, by offering new opportunities and necessitating the adaptation of the workforce to new roles where human intelligence and emotional understanding are irreplaceable.

However, it does not mean the change is imminent. As Roser (2023) shows, using data from Stein-Perlman et al.'s (2022) survey, there is no consensus among experts regarding the timeframe for developing AGI. Some are of the opinion that this level of technology will never be achievable. Others believe that it is possible, but it will take a considerable amount of time. However, many experts believe that it

Table 1.1 Comparison of ANI, AGI and ASI

Characteristic	ANI	AGI	ASI
Learning capability	Specialised learning within a specific domain.	Learns from diverse experiences across a wide range of domains.	Surpasses human ability to learn and improve, acquiring knowledge at an unprecedented scale.
Understanding and reasoning	Limited to understanding and reasoning within its programmed domain.	Comprehends context, makes judgements, and applies reasoning broadly, similar to human intelligence.	Exceeds human cognitive abilities, offering deep insights and solving complex problems beyond human comprehension.
Adaptability	Performs well in predefined tasks but struggles with unexpected changes.	Adapts to new, unforeseen circumstances and dynamically applies knowledge.	Exhibits superior adaptability, predicting and shaping the environment in ways unimaginable to humans.
Generalisation	Cannot generalise its knowledge to other domains beyond its training.	Generalises knowledge from one domain to another, leveraging insights across contexts.	Achieves ultimate generalisation, integrating and innovating across all domains of knowledge.
Scope of intelligence	Domain-specific intelligence with a narrow focus.	Comparable to a human's cognitive abilities across a broad range of functions.	Far exceeds any human intelligence, with capabilities spanning all conceivable domains and beyond.
Creation and innovation	Limited to optimising and improving within its specific domain without genuine innovation.	Capable of creative thinking and innovation across multiple fields, similar to an intelligent human.	Possesses creativity and innovation that could lead to groundbreaking advancements beyond human imagination.
Autonomy	Operates under human-set parameters and control.	Has autonomy similar to that of a human, making independent decisions across various contexts.	Autonomous decision-making with the ability to redefine objectives and outcomes beyond human control or understanding.

(R)evolution of translation technology 23

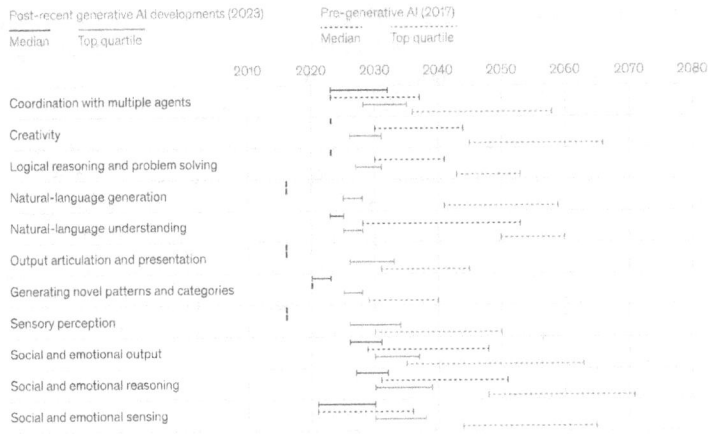

Figure 1.1 Estimated range for technology to achieve human-level performance, by technical capability.

Source: McKinsey & Company (2023).

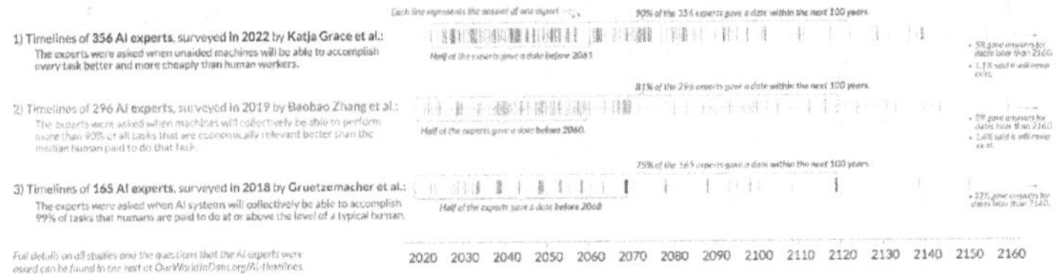

Figure 1.2 Median human-level AI estimate, (Roser, 2023), based on surveys conducted in 2018, 2019 and 2022.

Note: The median estimate is a statistical measure that represents the middle value in a set of predictions from experts. This means that half of the experts predict that human-level AI will be achieved before this year, and half predict it will be achieved after. The purpose of the median estimate is to summarise a wide range of expert opinions into a single, more easily interpretable figure. However, it is important to note that these estimates are highly speculative and depend on various factors, including advancements in technology, ethical considerations, regulatory environments and the allocation of resources for AI research and development (see Armstrong & Sotala, 2012; Grace et al., 2018).

can be developed in the next few decades (see the above figure; for more information see Stein-Perlman et al., 2022; Zhang et al., 2022). However, a noticeable trend is that the advancements in technology affect experts' expectations significantly.

The prospect of reaching ASI, an AI that surpasses human intelligence in all fields, including creativity, general wisdom and problem-solving, is even more speculative and futuristic. Such an advancement would not only mimic human capabilities but significantly exceed them, leading to innovations and decision-making on a level incomprehensible to humans. The ethical implications, risks and governance of ASI are subjects of intense debate and speculation, highlighting the importance of careful consideration and planning as we advance in AI development.

While the current stage of AI development presents remarkable capabilities, there is significant room for improvement and advancement. The potential journey towards AGI and ASI offers both exciting opportunities and formidable challenges. As AI continues to evolve, it is crucial for society, including professionals whose fields are directly impacted by AI, such as translators, to engage in continuous learning, adapt to new technologies and actively participate in shaping the future of AI to ensure that it aligns with ethical standards and human values. This will enable us to harness the benefits of AI while mitigating risks and ensuring that technology augmentation enhances human capabilities and contributes to further development of the profession, rather than replacing translators altogether.

The authors discuss the stages of AI development early in the book for several reasons. The discussion lays the foundation for understanding the profound implications of AI on the translator profession. This exploration seems valid here as it grounds the discussion in later chapters on augmented translation in hybrid workflows (Section 2.1), collaboration with AI systems (Section 2.2) and the impact of these advancements on translator profession (Section 2.3). Outlining the stages of AI development allows for anticipating future trends in translation technology and comprehending the dynamic nature of translator-AI interaction and the evolving skill sets required of translators, as discussed in Chapter 3 and beyond. The discussion hopefully sets the context for addressing the research findings (Chapter 4) and grounds the discussion on integrating AI and human expertise in translator training (Chapter 5).

References

Altman, Sam. 2023. 'Planning for AGI and Beyond'. 24 February 2023. https://openai.com/blog/planning-for-agi-and-beyond/.
Austermuhl, Frank. 2001. *Electronic Tools for Translators*. London: Routledge. https://doi.org/10.4324/9781315760353.
Baker, Mona, and Gabriela Saldanha, eds. 2019. *Routledge Encyclopedia of Translation Studies*. 3rd ed. London: Routledge. https://doi.org/10.4324/9781315678627.
Barrett, Anthony M., and Seth D. Baum. 2017. 'Risk Analysis and Risk Management for the Artificial Superintelligence Research and Development Process'. In *The Technological Singularity: Managing the Journey*, edited by Victor Callaghan, James Miller, Roman Yampolskiy, and Stuart Armstrong, 127–40. Berlin, Heidelberg: Springer. https://doi.org/10.1007/978-3-662-54033-6_6.
Baum, Seth, Anthony Barrett, and Roman V. Yampolskiy. 2017. 'Modeling and Interpreting Expert Disagreement About Artificial Superintelligence'. *SSRN Scholarly Paper*. Rochester, NY. https://papers.ssrn.com/abstract=3104645.
Becher, Johann Joachim. 1962. *Zur mechanischen Sprachübersetzung: ein Programmierungsversuch aus dem Jahre 1661: allgemeine Verschlüsselung der Sprachen (Character, pro Notitia Linguarum Universali) deutsch-lateinisch*. Stuttgart: W. Kohlhammer.
Bentivogli, Luisa, Beatrice Savoldi, Matteo Negri, Mattia Antonino Di Gangi, Roldano Cattoni, and Marco Turchi. 2020. 'Gender in Danger? Evaluating Speech Translation Technology on the MuST-SHE Corpus'. *arXiv*. https://doi.org/10.48550/arXiv.2006.05754.
Bostrom, Nick. 2014. *Superintelligence: Paths, Dangers, Strategies*. Oxford University Press.
Bostrom, Nick, and Eliezer Yudkowsky. 2014. 'The Ethics of Artificial Intelligence'. In *The Cambridge Handbook of Artificial Intelligence*, edited by Keith Frankish and William M. Ramsey, 316–34. Cambridge: Cambridge University Press. https://doi.org/10.1017/CBO9781139046855.020.
Bowker, Lynne. 2002. *Computer-Aided Translation Technology: A Practical Introduction*. University of Ottawa Press.
Bowker, Lynne, and Des Fischer. 2010. 'Computer-Aided Translation'. In *Handbook of Translation Studies*, edited by Yves Gambier and Luc van Doorslaer, 60–65. John Benjamins Publishing.
Brooks, Rodney. 2017. '[FoR&AI] Domo Arigato Mr. Roboto'. Robots, AI, and Other Stuff. 28 August 2017. https://rodneybrooks.com/forai-domo-arigato-mr-roboto/.
Brynjolfsson, Erik, and Andrew McAfee. 2014. *The Second Machine Age: Work, Progress, and Prosperity in a Time of Brilliant Technologies*.

The Second Machine Age: Work, Progress, and Prosperity in a Time of Brilliant Technologies. New York: WW Norton.
Bundy, Alan. 2017. 'Preparing for the Future of Artificial Intelligence'. *AI & Society* 32 (2): 285–87. https://doi.org/10.1007/s00146-016-0685-0.
Camgoz, Necati Cihan, Oscar Koller, Simon Hadfield, and Richard Bowden. 2020. 'Sign Language Transformers: Joint End-to-End Sign Language Recognition and Translation'. *arXiv*. https://doi.org/10.48550/arXiv.2003.13830.
Cao, Yihan, Siyu Li, Yixin Liu, Zhiling Yan, Yutong Dai, Philip S. Yu, and Lichao Sun. 2023. 'A Comprehensive Survey of AI-Generated Content (AIGC): A History of Generative AI from GAN to ChatGPT'. *Journal of ACM* 37 (4). https://doi.org/10.48550/arXiv.2303.04226.
Chan, Sin-wai. 2004. *A Dictionary of Translation Technology*. Hong Kong: Chinese University Press.
Chan, Sin-wai. 2015. *The Routledge Encyclopedia of Translation Technology*. Routledge.
Costa-Jussà, Marta R., Mireia Farrús, José B. Mariño, and José A. R. Fonollosa. 2012. 'Study and Comparison of Rule-Based and Statistical Catalan-Spanish Machine Translation Systems'. *Computing and Informatics* 31 (2): 245–70.
Frankenberg-Garcia, Ana, Robert Lew, Geraint Paul Rees, Jonathan C. Roberts, and Nirwan Sharma. 2019. 'Developing a Writing Assistant to Help Eap Writers with Collocations in Real Time'. *ReCALL* 31 (1): 23–39. https://doi.org/10.1017/S0958344018000150.
Garcia, Ignatio. 2015. 'Computer-Aided Translation Systems'. In *Routledge Encyclopedia of Translation Technology*, edited by Sin-wai Chan, 68–87. Amsterdam and Philadelphia: Routledge.
Gayed, John Maurice, May Kristine Jonson Carlon, Angelu Mari Oriola, and Jeffrey S. Cross. 2022. 'Exploring an Ai-Based Writing Assistant's Impact on English Language Learners'. *Computers and Education: Artificial Intelligence* 3 (January): 100055. https://doi.org/10.1016/j.caeai.2022.100055.
Gemert, Igor van. 2023. 'What's Next in AI (10 Stages)'. LinkedIn. 2023. https://t.ly/GdTBh.
George, Andrew R. 2003. *The Babylonian Gilgamesh Epic: Introduction, Critical Edition and Cuneiform Texts – Volume 1*. Oxford: Oxford University Press.
Godwin-Jones, Robert. 2022. 'Partnering with Ai: Intelligent Writing Assistance and Instructed Language Learning'. https://hdl.handle.net/10125/73474.
Goertzel, Ben, and Cassio Pennachin. 2007. *Artificial General Intelligence*. Springer.
Grace, Katja, John Salvatier, Allan Dafoe, Baobao Zhang, and Owain Evans. 2018. 'Viewpoint: When Will AI Exceed Human Performance? Evidence

from AI Experts'. *Journal of Artificial Intelligence Research* 62 (July): 729–54. https://doi.org/10.1613/jair.1.11222.

Green, Spence, Jeffrey Heer, and Christopher D. Manning. 2015. 'Natural Language Translation at the Intersection of AI and HCI'. *Acmqueue*. http://queue.acm.org/detail.cfm?id=2798086.

Groves, Michael, and Klaus Mundt. 2015. 'Friend or Foe? Google Translate in Language for Academic Purposes'. *English for Specific Purposes* 37 (January): 112–21. https://doi.org/10.1016/j.esp.2014.09.001.

Herbert, Sarah, Félix do Carmo, Joanna Gough, and Anu Carnegie-Brown. 2023. 'From Responsibilities to Responsibility: A Study of the Effects of Translation Workflow Automation'. *Journal of Specialised Translation* 40: 9–35.

Hutchins, John. 1995. 'Machine Translation: A Brief History'. In *Concise History of the Language Sciences: From the Sumerians to the Cognitivists*, edited by Ernst F. K. Koerner and Ronald E. Asher, 431–45. Oxford: Pergamon Press.

———. 1997. 'First Steps in Mechanical Translation'. In Machine Translation Summit. www.hutchinsweb.me.uk/MTS-1997.pdf.

———. 2006. 'Machine Translation: History'. In *Encyclopedia of Language and Linguistics*, edited by Keith Brown, 375–83. Boston, MA: Elsevier.

———. 2010. 'Machine Translation: A Concise History'. *Journal of Translation Studies* 13 (1–2): 29–70.

James, Alex. 2021. 'The Why, What, and How of Artificial General Intelligence Chip Development'. *IEEE Transactions on Cognitive and Developmental Systems* 13 (3): 1–29. https://ieeexplore.ieee.org/abstract/document/9390376/

Jiang, Kai, and Xi Lu. 2021. 'The Influence of Speech Translation Technology on Interpreter's Career Prospects in the Era of Artificial Intelligence'. *Journal of Physics: Conference Series* 1802 (4): 042074. https://doi.org/10.1088/1742-6596/1802/4/042074.

Jimenez-Crespo, Miguel A. 2013. Translation and Web Localization. Routledge. https://doi.org/10.4324/9780203520208.

Jungherr, Andreas. 2023. 'Artificial Intelligence and Democracy: A Conceptual Framework'. *Social Media + Society* 9 (3): 20563051231186353. https://doi.org/10.1177/20563051231186353.

Kelly, Louis G. 1995. 'History of Translation'. In *Concise History of the Language Sciences: From the Sumerians to the Cognitivists*, edited by Ernst F. K. Koerner and Ronald E. Asher, 419–30. Oxford: Pergamon Press.

Kenny, Dorothy. 2011. 'Electronic Tools and Resources for Translators'. In *The Oxford Handbook of Translation Studies*, edited by Kirsten Malmkjær and Kevin Windle, 455–72. Oxford University Press. https://doi.org/10.1093/oxfordhb/9780199239306.013.0031.

Khurana, Diksha, Aditya Koli, Kiran Khatter, and Sukhdev Singh. 2023. 'Natural Language Processing: State of the Art, Current Trends and

Challenges'. *Multimedia Tools and Applications* 82: 3713–44. https://doi.org/10.1007/s11042-022-13428-4.

Koehn, Philipp. 2009. *Statistical Machine Translation*. Cambridge: Cambridge University Press.

Kong, Linghui. 2022. '[Retracted] Artificial Intelligence-Based Translation Technology in Translation Teaching'. Edited by Arpit Bhardwaj. *Computational Intelligence and Neuroscience* 2022 (June): 6016752. https://doi.org/10.1155/2022/6016752.

Kornacki, Michał. 2018. *Computer-Assisted Translation (CAT) Tools in the Translator Training Process*. Berlin: Peter Lang.

Kurzweil, Ray. 2005. *The Singularity Is Near: When Humans Transcend Biology*. Viking.

Long, Lynne. 2007. 'History and Translation'. In *A Companion to Translation Studies*, edited by Piotr Kuhwiczak and Karin Littau, 63–76. Toronto: Multilingual Matters.

Lopez, Adam. 2008. 'Statistical Machine Translation'. *ACM Comput. Surv.* 40 (3). https://doi.org/10.1145/1380584.1380586.

McKinsey and Company. 2023. 'What Is the Future of Generative AI?' Accessed 11 February 2024. www.mckinsey.com/featured-insights/mckinsey-explainers/whats-the-future-of-generative-ai-an-early-view-in-15-charts.

Melby, Alan K. 2019. 'Future of Machine Translation: Musings on Weaver's Memo'. In *The Routledge Handbook of Translation and Technology*, edited by Minako O'Hagan, 1–20. London: Routledge. www.ttt.org/wp-content/uploads/2022/05/MT-Weaver-v1a.pdf.

Mucci, Tim, and Cole Stryker. 2023. 'What Is Artificial-Superintelligence?' 18 December 2023. www.ibm.com/topics/artificial-superintelligence.

Newell, Allen, and Herbert A. Simon. 1976. 'Computer Science as Empirical Inquiry: Symbols and Search'. *Commun. ACM* 19 (3): 113–26. https://doi.org/10.1145/360018.360022.

Olohan, Maeve. 2015. Scientific and Technical Translation. London: Routledge. https://doi.org/10.4324/9781315679600.

'Phrase TMS (CAT Tool)'. 2024. Phrase. Accessed 13 July 2024. https://support.phrase.com/hc/en-us/articles/5709660879516-Phrase-Language-AI-TMS

Pietrzak, Paulina, and Michał Kornacki. 2021. *Using CAT Tools in Freelance Translation: Insights from a Case Study*. London: Routledge. https://doi.org/10.4324/9781003125761.

Pokrivcakova, Silvia. 2019. 'Preparing Teachers for the Application of AI-Powered Technologies in Foreign Language Education'. *Journal of Language and Cultural Education* 7 (3): 135–53.

Pooley, David. 2023. 'Preparing for Take-off: How AI Will Turbocharge Translation Engines'. https://trados.com/blog/preparing-for-take-off-how-ai-will-turbo-charge-translation-engines/.

Pym, Anthony. 2023. *Exploring Translation Theories*. London: Routledge.
Roser, Max. 2023. 'AI Timelines: What Do Experts in Artificial Intelligence Expect for the Future?' *Our World in Data*.
Russell, Stuart, and Peter Norvig. 2021. *Artificial Intelligence: A Modern Approach, 4th Ed.* Harlow: Pearson.
Sarsia, Pankaj, Satyam Mishra, Aradhya Joshi, Amit Agrawal, and Shristi Mishra. 2023. 'Unveiling the Neural Mirage in the Pursuit of Transcendent Intelligence'. *Engineering Proceedings* 59 (1). https://doi.org/10.3390/engproc2023059102.
Somers, Harold, ed. 2003. *Computers and Translation. Btl.35*. John Benjamins Publishing. https://benjamins.com/catalog/btl.35.
Stein-Perlman, Zach, Benjamin Weinstein-Raun, and Katja Grace. 2022. '2022 Expert Survey on Progress in AI'. *AI Impacts*. 3 August 2022. https://aiimpacts.org/2022-expert-survey-on-progress-in-ai/.
Vieira, Lucas Nunes. 2020. 'Automation Anxiety and Translators'. *Translation Studies* 13 (1): 1–21. https://doi.org/10.1080/14781700.2018.1543613.
Vieira, Lucas Nunes, Minako O'Hagan, and Carol O'Sullivan. 2021. 'Understanding the Societal Impacts of Machine Translation: A Critical Review of the Literature on Medical and Legal Use Cases'. *Information, Communication & Society* 24 (11): 1515–32. https://doi.org/10.1080/1369118X.2020.1776370.
Windle, Kevin, and Anthony Pym. 2011. '7 European Thinking on Secular Translation'. In *The Oxford Handbook of Translation Studies*, edited by Kirsten Malmkjær and Kevin Windle, 7–22. Oxford University Press. https://doi.org/10.1093/oxfordhb/9780199239306.013.0002.
Yampolskiy, Roman V. 2015. Artificial Superintelligence: A Futuristic Approach. 1st edition. Chapman and Hall/CRC. https://doi.org/10.1201/b18612.
Zanettin, Federico. 2012. *Translation-Driven Corpora: Corpus Resources for Descriptive and Applied Translation Studies*. St. Jerome Publishing.
Zhang, Baobao, Noemi Dreksler, Markus Anderljung, Lauren Kahn, Charlie Giattino, Allan Dafoe, and Michael C. Horowitz. 2022. 'Forecasting AI Progress: Evidence from a Survey of Machine Learning Researchers'. *arXiv*. https://doi.org/10.48550/arXiv.2206.04132.

2 Translator–AI interaction

2.1 Augmented translation

The significance of AI in translation extends beyond simply efficiency. Machine learning has revolutionised the translation industry by significantly enhancing productivity and ensuring better consistency in translation. Automated translation systems have challenged traditional notions of translation. While AI-powered systems can handle the mechanical aspects of translation, such as terminology consistency, glossary creation and rapid translation of large volumes of text, they struggle with pragmatic translation, domain expertise and understanding context (Lumeras & Way, 2017). Human translators, on the other hand, excel in these areas thanks to their nuanced understanding, creativity and cultural sensitivity.

Therefore, the most successful human-AI interaction translation workflows involve a complementary dynamic, where AI supports the mechanical aspects of translation, freeing human translators to focus on the more complex, nuanced aspects of language that machines cannot yet replicate. This convergence of technology and human expertise enables the handling of increasing volumes of content necessitated by globalisation and the digital age, where information exchange is paramount. Moorkens and O'Brien (2017) suggest that successful collaboration between humans and machines in translation tasks depends on developing interfaces that facilitate easy post-editing, offer customisable features and integrate effectively with both TM and MT outputs. This integration of AI into translation workflows prompts a re-evaluation of the skills and roles of human translators. Rather than rendering human translators obsolete, AI has the potential to augment their work, freeing them from the task of translating routine, repetitive content and allowing them to focus on complex, nuanced and creative aspects of translation.

Engelbart (1962) introduced the concept of augmenting human intellect, emphasising the enhancement of a person's capability to tackle complex situations, improve comprehension, and devise solutions more effectively. This concept entails not only quicker and better comprehension but also the ability to understand previously incomprehensible situations, leading to faster and superior solutions, including solving previously unsolvable problems.

O'Brien (2023) observes that human performance is limited by cognitive load, suggesting that augmentation can transcend this barrier and enhance intelligence by leveraging technologies related to human perception and cognitive function. Alicea (2018) and Stanney et al. (2015) support this view, highlighting the potential of augmentation to extend human capabilities. Raisamo et al. (2019) further elucidate this concept by illustrating how augmented human combines elements of augmented reality (AR), virtual reality (VR), ubiquitous computing, and other user interface paradigms in innovative ways. Consequently, human augmentation is portrayed as a comprehensive integration of various factors that collectively improve performance and interaction with the work environment, as suggested by Martin et al. (2011) and Salmi et al. (2017). This holistic approach to augmentation underscores its potential to significantly impact human engagement with their professional surroundings.

In the field of translation, the practice has evolved into an augmented activity through the adoption of universal tools and technologies (Jiménez-Crespo, 2023; O'Brien, 2023). Lommel (2020) discusses the introduction of the concept of "augmented translation" by CSA Research in 2017, defining it as a technology-centric approach aimed at enhancing the capabilities of human translators. This initiative anticipated the gradual integration of additional technologies to establish an AI-driven platform for linguists. Such a platform is designed to significantly increase efficiency and proficiency by automating repetitive tasks and minimising disruptions associated with information retrieval. This forward-looking perspective underscores the evolving role of technology in transforming the translation profession towards greater productivity and effectiveness.

Lommel (2020) outlines several key technological components of augmented translation:

- **Adaptive Neural Machine Translation.** NMT, built on deep-learning algorithms and large datasets, has shown remarkable improvements over previous statistical methods, offering translations that are often more fluent and coherent (Sutskever et al., 2014; Vaswani et al., 2023). The adaptive aspect of this technology enables it to tailor its operations to the specific content being translated, learning the terminology and stylistic preferences unique to each translator. By remembering the nuances of translations at the sub-segment level, it extends beyond traditional translation memory systems, offering unprecedented support in translating previously unseen texts in a manner that aligns with the individual translator's methodologies (DePalma, 2017).
- **Lights-out Project Management** represents a paradigm in which projects are executed via a touchless, self-service model, significantly reducing the necessity for project manager intervention. Lommel (2020) explains that this automation-centric approach ensures that processes are streamlined unless an issue necessitates human oversight. The advantages of such a methodology are multifaceted, including accelerated project initiation, enhanced transparency for stakeholders and a comprehensive assurance that all elements of a project are meticulously managed. This innovative approach to project management not only optimises operational efficiency but also fosters a more reliable and transparent interaction with clients.
- **Integration of Translation Memory and Machine Translation** is pivotal in creating a system that enhances real-time learning by assimilating human feedback and analysing linguist interactions. Lommel (2020) states that mere reliance on MT is insufficient for augmenting human capabilities. However, when MT evolves by adapting to the inputs from linguists on individual and collective levels, it leads to a seamless integration with TM. This dynamic interaction not only blurs the distinctions between TM and MT but also narrows the gap between human and machine capabilities, facilitating a more collaborative and efficient translation process.
- **Terminology Management and Automated Content Enrichment (ACE)** necessitate the use of applications that integrate terminology with knowledge management. Weber (2018) points out how

ACE aids translators by providing clarifications for ambiguous terms and facilitating the localisation of content across diverse cultures. This process is intricately linked to terminology management through the utilisation of a comprehensive terminology database. The availability of terminology enriched with detailed metadata significantly enhances the accuracy and contextuality of both human and machine translations, leading to outputs that are consistently precise and culturally appropriate (Lommel, 2020).

Figure 2.1 shows CSA 2020s a technology-centric approach to amplifying the capabilities of human translators.

However, the above seems incomplete without mentioning GenAI. Therefore, it is proposed here that an additional section dedicated to GenAI be included in the analysis.

- **GenAI Translation**, which utilises the large language model (LLM) Transformer architecture, a cutting-edge approach that facilitates the generation of human-like responses within conversational contexts. This technology employs sophisticated deep-learning algorithms to produce natural language responses to given input texts, effectively mirroring human linguistic abilities (Haque

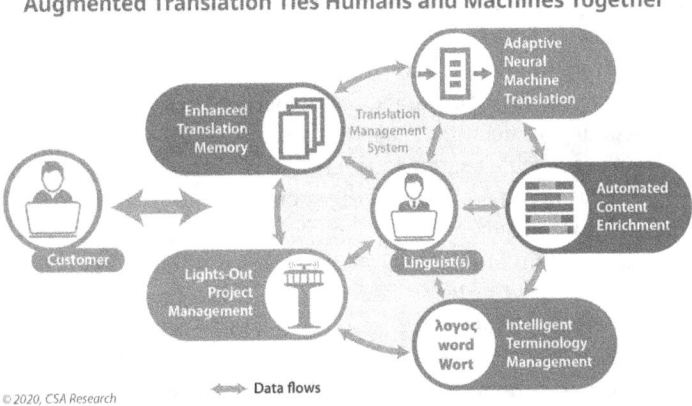

Figure 2.1 Augmented translation ties humans and machines together.

Source: Lommel, 2020.

& Li, 2024). Such capabilities enable the translation of texts in response to specific prompts, demonstrating the potential of GenAI translation to revolutionise the field by offering nuanced, context-aware translations. (see Section 2.2).

The concept of augmentation extends beyond the mere process of translation. As previously discussed, human augmentation integrates various factors that collectively enhance performance and interaction with the environment (Martin et al., 2011; Salmi et al., 2017; O'Brien, 2023). Consequently, augmented translation necessitates the emergence of a new breed of professional, termed the "augmented translator" by DePalma (2017) and CSA Research. These professionals operate within a technologically advanced environment designed to automate the execution of routine tasks, thereby freeing up their time and energy. This environment ensures that pertinent information is readily accessible, enhancing the consistency, responsiveness and productivity of language professionals. Thus, augmented translators can devote their attention to the more nuanced and engaging aspects of their work, moving beyond the mechanical aspects of translation.

Nevertheless, the adoption of augmented translation introduces several challenges. The integration of AI tools into established translation processes necessitates considerable technological investments and extensive training for translators to harness these tools proficiently. Incorporating AI into the translation workflow mandates a solid grasp of both the potential and the limitations inherent in these technologies. NMT systems, for example, have achieved significant advancements in producing translations that are both fluent and contextually precise (Sutskever et al., 2014). Yet, the performance of these systems is critically contingent upon the quality and scope of the training data, as well as the available computational resources.

Consequently, the effective utilisation of AI tools within translation workflows requires the development of a comprehensive training program for translators. Such programs must address the technical use of AI tools and foster an in-depth understanding of how to seamlessly integrate human expertise with AI functionalities to optimise outcomes. It is imperative that translators are equipped with the necessary skills to monitor and refine AI-generated outputs, ensuring the translations adhere to the highest standards of accuracy, nuance and cultural appropriateness (Haque & Li, 2024). Moreover, the integration of AI into translation processes introduces a variety of ethical and social implications (Section 2.4). It also highlights new areas of interest for translation scholars and translator educators. The demand for high-quality and accurate AI-generated translations necessitates comprehensive quality assurance protocols. Stringent quality assurance measures play a crucial role in upholding the quality and fidelity of translations, a factor that necessitates careful consideration within the framework of translation studies and translation education (see Chapter 3).

In conclusion, the progression towards augmented translation marks a significant phase in the field of linguistics, driven by the integration of artificial intelligence and technological advancements. This transformation, rooted in Engelbart's (1962) foundational concept of augmenting human intellect, is evolving to enhance translation practices significantly, offering a blend of efficiency, accuracy and nuanced understanding previously unattainable. The adoption of adaptive neural machine translation, lights-out project management and sophisticated terminology management systems, as suggested by DePalma (2017) and Lommel (2020), represents a leap forward in thinking about how translations can be approached, enabling translators to work more effectively and focus on the intricacies that define linguistic excellence. However, the transition to an augmented translation paradigm necessitates careful navigation of the challenges it presents, including the need for substantial investment in technology and training as well as addressing ethical considerations. The potential of augmented translation to revolutionise the industry is immense, promising a future where the symbiosis of human expertise and machine intelligence leads to unparalleled linguistic achievements. Yet, the success of this endeavour will rely on a balanced approach that honours the complexity of language and the human touch that remains irreplaceable.

2.2 Hybrid workflows in translation

Hybrid workflows in translation represent an approach that synergises human expertise with MT technologies (memoQ, online), aiming to balance the speed and efficiency of MT with the nuanced understanding and interpretive skills of human translators. Gurov (2023) discusses the impact of artificial intelligence on the translator's role, highlighting the changes in the translation process where hybrid workflows play a crucial role in maintaining quality while managing the increased volume and speed demands.

The concept of hybrid workflows addresses several key challenges in translation, including the need for rapid turnaround times without compromising the quality of translated content. Machine translation offers the advantage of quickly processing large volumes of text but often lacks the ability to fully capture the subtleties of language, such as cultural nuances, idiomatic expressions and context-specific meanings (Hutchins & Somers, 1992; Koehn, 2009). On the other hand, human translators excel in these areas but cannot match the speed of machines. Therefore, the hybrid approach aims to harness the strengths of both, using machines for initial translations and humans for refinement and validation, ensuring the final product is both accurate and culturally appropriate (O'Brien, 2012). The list below presents major elements of human-machine collaboration and how they may work together in hybrid workflows:

- machine translation: this is the use of software to translate text from one language to another automatically; however, it may not always handle nuances, idiomatic expressions or technical terms accurately;
- human translation: human translators bring linguistic expertise, cultural knowledge and the ability to understand context and subtleties in language;
- pre-editing: in some workflows, human input is used before machine translation to standardise text, remove ambiguities and make it more machine-translation-friendly in order to improve the quality of the machine-translated output;
- post-editing: this involves human translators reviewing and correcting machine-translated content;
- TM and glossaries: these tools support both machine and human translation processes, seamlessly allowing the integration of human and machine effort.

The hybrid model is not static; it continuously evolves with technological advancements. As machine learning algorithms become more sophisticated, the role of human translators shifts towards more specialised tasks, such as editing, proofreading and ensuring that translations meet the specific requirements of the target audience. An example of such a change is the introduction of GenAI translation workflow, potentially shifting the role of human translators even more.

GenAI translation workflow utilises generative capabilities of both publicly and commercially available LLMs (e.g., ChatGPT by OpenAI). In a GenAI-based translation scenario, the translator uses an LLM to translate a text. Most LLMs interact with users through a web-based interface, where each user input to the LLM is referred to as a "prompt". Unlike MT, GenAI necessitates the provision of specific prompts from users to guide the output generation, ensuring the model aligns with the intended task or output expectation.

The idea of prompting allows translators to have their text translated according to pre-set conditions, like using certain spelling conventions, word usage, target audience or context provided by the translator. Below, the authors present a simple prompt to be used in the case of medical translation:

```
You are an expert translator of medical texts from Polish to
English. Please translate the text provided at the bottom of
this prompt. Please consider the following data:

[STYLE GUIDANCE]
Please consider source and target sentences from a similar
section of a similar document. Refer to this for general style
and terminology.
[No data to share at this time.]

Please take into consideration the revised translation to be
found below:
[No data to share at this time.]

[SPECIFIC INSTRUCTIONS]
Please follow these project-specific instructions:
[No data to share at this time.]

[TERMINOLOGY]
Use this glossary when translating:
[No data to share at this time.]

Translate this:
```

Using this prompt, a translator can submit the text to be translated alongside the extra information (context, style, terminology, other) that the system needs to generate a translation closer to the translator's expectations than in the case of unprompted MT. GenAI workflow is not limited to translation only. Translators can use a wide variety of prompts to process text according to their needs, e.g. terminology mining:

```
Please act as an expert terminologist.
Extract specialised terms from the provided text and translate them into Polish.
Present the translations in a specific format where the source term is listed first, followed by a tabulator, and then the target term. For example, if the source term is "white", it should be presented as "white[tabulator]biały".
Render Polish terms in nominative case.
Sort terms alphabetically.
Please consider [SPECIAL INSTRUCTIONS] if given.

[SPECIAL INSTRUCTIONS]

Text:
```

This simple prompt allows the translator to mine a text for specialised terminology (LLM does not know what is "specialised" unless the translator teaches it, hence [SPECIAL INSTRUCTIONS]), translate it and produce the result in a format that allows the content to be copied into any spreadsheet tool (tabulator separates the text into two columns by default), and then easily import it into most CAT tools (or keep as a reference for future GenAI translations). A person's actual needs and imagination limit the number of applications.

It must be stressed here that the GenAI translation workflow demonstrated above serves as merely one instance of a hybrid model, in which human involvement is not limited to initial input through prompts. Rigorous human oversight is indispensable at both preprocessing and post-processing stages when interacting with LLMs to secure optimal translation quality and fidelity. This comprehensive engagement ensures that the translation output aligns with the highest standards of accuracy and textual contextuality.

Another example of GenAI-powered workflow is that proposed by Steven Bammer, called Generative AI Iterative Translation (GAIT) (Bammel, 2023). This type of workflow represents an innovative approach to translation that leverages the capabilities of GenAI to enhance the translation process at the translator level even more than in the case of simple prompting an LLM. This approach, which integrates specialised LLM-client software, underscores the evolving nature of translation as a revision-centric activity, departing from the conventional static workflows dominated by Machine Translation Post-Editing (MTPE) practices.

GAIT is a translation process that involves a collaboration between human translators and GenAI technologies. The process is designed to optimise the translation process using AI. It begins by creating an "anchor prompt" that guides the AI, followed by translating text batches. The AI-generated outputs are then refined by human translators, and the anchor prompt is updated based on these edits to improve future translations. This iterative loop aims to leverage the strengths of both human expertise and AI capabilities, resulting in a translation process that improves with each iteration (see also Wu et al., 2022).

To sum up, hybrid workflows in translation synergise human expertise with MT technologies, aiming to blend the speed of MT with human translators' nuanced understanding. This approach addresses the need for quick, quality translations by combining automatic software translation with human refinement and validation, ensuring accuracy and cultural appropriateness. The methodology of hybrid workflows evolves with technology, notably with GenAI, shifting translators' roles towards more specialised tasks and allowing for customised translations through specific prompts, exemplifying modern translation workflows' dynamic and collaborative nature.

2.3 The impact of technology on translator profession: new avenues and new anxieties

The profession of the translator has been subject to many radical changes over the last 50 years. Computerisation, the expansion of the Internet, the development of technologies such as TMS, MT and finally AI have all made a profound impact not only on how translators translate, but also on how they approach new projects. These technological advancements have altered their project management strategies, collaboration methods, organisational practices and efficiency in optimising the ratio of time spent to benefits gained. All these changes have significantly transformed the daily work and workflows of translators in professional settings (see McDonough, 2007; O'Brien & Rossetti, 2020).

As observed by Mossop (2006: 791), what "is new here is not technological change per se but a change in the way humans are organised to do work". Indeed, TMS tools are now routinely employed for project management, aiding collaboration and ensuring version control. The incorporation of MT has automated repetitive tasks in translation, often expediting the initial stages of content translation. The introduction of AI admittedly enables the translator to enhance productivity in their daily tasks. Language processing has become more nuanced and context-aware than ever before. Although its use may seem controversial and stirs debates in the translation industry, translators are increasingly employing AI to facilitate their work and streamline the translation process, enhance linguistic accuracy and improve overall efficiency.

The rapidly evolving AI technology has offered transformative potential for practical aspects of the profession. Before acknowledging the challenges that accompany these advancements, it needs to be admitted that AI can revolutionise translation. The opportunities presented by AI technologies are primarily attributed to their capacity for processing large datasets (see section 1.1.5). Moreover, AI's application of machine learning algorithms enables the continuous improvement of translation quality through the analysis of vast amounts of language data. This capacity not only speeds up the translation process but also enhances the precision and reliability of translated texts. AI-driven translation tools that incorporate algorithms that can understand and translate context-specific aspects of language represent a notable advancement over traditional translation methods, which may struggle with such complexities.

It is crucial, however, to approach these developments with a critical perspective, examining the potential challenges and ethical implications they introduce. Although automation can often be perceived as a positive change, relieving translators of routine tasks, in fact – as Herbert et al. (2023: 29) note – "professionals may well prefer to have more responsibilities in certain cases, as this can hold various values for them in relation to a sense of control and job satisfaction". Given such circumstances, the integration of AI in translation necessitates ongoing research and dialogue to ensure that these technologies are implemented in a manner that balances enthusiasm for these advancements with careful consideration of their limitations and implications.

Among the challenges posed by advancements in this field, some relate to the translation product and process, while others impact the translation profession. The challenges associated with the very product of translation primarily revolve around maintaining accuracy, consistency and cultural sensitivity across translated materials. In hybrid translation workflows, which incorporate AI technologies, there is an increased risk of losing subtle semantic nuance and context. This phenomenon is attributable to the inherent limitations of current AI models in fully understanding and replicating the complexity of human languages and cultural contexts. Since translation goes beyond managing the complexities of the working languages, each with its unique grammatical structures, lexical peculiarities and cultural nuances, ensuring that the target text is not only linguistically accurate but also culturally appropriate and sensitive may not always be feasible for AI technologies as it requires a deep cultural and contextual awareness (Hutchins & Somers, 1992; Koehn, 2009) (see section 2.2).

Regarding the second type of challenges introduced by AI technologies, the issues affecting the translation profession encompass a broad spectrum of concerns. This involves a significant transformation in translation workflows, among other concerns. The translation industry, like many others, is in a state of flux due to technological advancements. The impact of AI on translation workflows and efficiency is so profound that, in fact, most translation jobs nowadays do not start from scratch; instead, translators receive pre-translated documents that require post-editing (see Krings & Koby, 2001; O'Brien, 2007; Guerberof Arenas, 2013; Guerberof-Arenas & Moorkens, 2023). It may soon be that most jobs will not require translation but rather post-editing.

Therefore, the challenges posed by AI technologies to translator professions as such include the evolving role of translators in the face of increasingly sophisticated AI tools, which necessitate a shift towards roles that emphasise editing, post-editing and quality assurance. The redefinition of translators' roles and responsibilities (see Schäffner 2020; Risku et al., 2021; Ehrensberger-Dow et al., 2023) highlights the necessity for translators to adapt, embracing new skills and approaches to their work (see Section 3.1). Therefore, there is a growing need for translators to develop skills in technology management and to adapt to new workflows that integrate human and machine efforts; such adaptation underscores the importance of flexibility and resilience among professionals facing the dynamic demands of the industry (see Section 3.4).

Failure to adapt could present yet another substantial challenge to the translation industry, potentially resulting in job losses for human translators. As these technological innovations automate tasks that were once solely dependent on human expertise, this progression towards automation may lead to a devaluation of human skill and expertise, possibly resulting in job displacement within the translation profession. Tomarenko (2019: 286) states that the threat of job loss due to automation for translators necessitates a shift in focus towards areas where their unique contributions are significant. As a countermeasure to the threats of automation, translators might strategically redirect their expertise towards more creative domains, capitalising on their nuanced comprehension of language and culture (Johnson, 2017). This approach positions their competencies in realms where AI continues to falter in emulating the depth of human creativity and emotional acuity.

It needs to be emphasised here, that – as observed by Carl (2020: 500) – "rather than representing the mechanisms of the human mind, MT systems are today more frequently considered automatised aides that extend human cognition". Indeed, rather than viewing AI as a threat, it can be seen as an opportunity for translators to adapt and enhance the future role of human translators (Lumeras & Way, 2017). As such, the translation profession faces a critical period of adaptation, requiring continuous professional development and a re-evaluation of traditional roles to ensure relevance and value in the digital age. Zhu (2023: online) states that,

> with its increasing application in all sectors of life, the use of artificial intelligence or machine translation is on its way to becoming mainstream in the translation industry, eliminating bread-winning opportunities from translators, leaving them in the stream of life to sink or swim.

The future may not be a matter of sinking or swimming, but rather learning how to navigate new waters, where AI is a tool that can be viewed as an asset to be utilised, not as a threat that makes human translators redundant.

This shift requires translators to reconsider their approach to their profession, focusing on how AI technologies can be integrated into their existing practices. By regarding AI not as a threat that makes human translators redundant, but as a means to enhance efficiency and accuracy, translators highlight their essential role. Their competence includes elements that AI cannot completely comprehend and manage, which underscores the complementary relationship between human expertise and technological advancement in translation, positioning human translators as vital in the age of AI.

2.4 Ethical considerations in AI-assisted language service provision

Following the examination of the opportunities and challenges presented by the ongoing AI revolution in the translation market, it seems crucial to explore ethical and professional considerations related to the integration of AI technologies into translation practices. The evolution of translation workflows due to technological advancements poses substantial ethical concerns (see Drugan, 2017; Kenny et al., 2020; Horváth, 2022). As Green (2020: online) puts it, "AI, as the externalisation of human intelligence, offers us in amplified form everything that humanity already is, both good and evil". This perspective on the dual nature of AI, as both a mirror and an amplifier of humanity's capabilities and flaws, necessitates a careful examination of AI's application in translation, ensuring that its deployment upholds ethical standards and maintains the integrity and professionalism of translation services.

One of the primary ethical concerns is data privacy. Numerous studies (DePalma, 2014; Bowker & Ciro, 2019; Canfora & Ottmann, 2020; Vieira et al., 2023) have extensively investigated the privacy issues associated with the use of MT in global research contexts, highlighting the potential risks involved in utilising online MT systems. Vieira et al. (2023: 25) emphasise the complexity of online machine translation (MT) systems, which are underpinned by extensive networks of information and communication technologies. When users engage with these systems to exchange information, there is an inherent risk that "the records they keep are inherently subject to exposure" (ibid.). This concern is amplified in the context of AI due to the unparalleled volume of information shared by users. The amount of data exchanged with AI systems introduces significant privacy and security considerations, underscoring the urgent need for data protection.

Since the use of AI-driven systems often involves processing highly confidential and sensitive data, it is imperative to consider the importance of safeguarding client data and ensuring that information remains secure. This involves scrutinising the data handling practices of AI tools and ensuring compliance with data protection regulations. It is, however, hard to control the access to and possession of the data so what is particularly concerning in the case of hybrid translation workflows is the issue of copyright infringement and the potential misuse of AI-generated translations. Bird et al. (2020: 2) argue that AI ethics "is concerned with the important question of how human developers, manufacturers and operators should behave in order to minimise the ethical harms that can arise from AI in society, either arising from poor (unethical) design, inappropriate application or misuse". The emphasis here is on fostering a responsible framework that guides the AI community in creating and deploying AI in a manner that minimally impacts society negatively, ensuring that ethical considerations are paramount in the evolution of AI systems.

This ethical issue extends well beyond focusing solely on client data confidentiality and protecting client privacy to also include personal and informational privacy of the user, in this case the translator (see van Dijk, 2012: 113). This type of privacy pertains to the user's capacity to regulate access to their own data, particularly with respect to personal or private information. It encompasses not only the safeguarding of tangible details but also extends to more nuanced aspects of the user's digital footprint, such as their tendencies, likes, preferences, dislikes, behavioural and emotional patterns. This multifaceted approach to privacy acknowledges the complex nature of digital identity, recognising that the essence of the user's private life is not limited to static data points but includes dynamic, behaviourally-driven information that paints a fuller picture of their personal sphere. The vulnerabilities within AI systems – which present potential security risks that could result in the exploitation of sensitive or confidential information – necessitate further exploration and intervention in the field of translation research and practice.

Another crucial ethical concern is the imperative for transparency in the use of AI and MT in translation processes (see Larsson et al., 2019). This is underscored by the ethical guidelines issued in April 2019 by the European Union Commission's High-Level Expert Group on Artificial Intelligence (AI HLEG), which delineates transparency as one of the seven pivotal requisites for the achievement of "trustworthy AI". This principle has also been prominently reflected in the Commission's White Paper on AI, emphasising the necessity for clear and open practices in AI applications. In hybrid translation workflows, clients have the right to know when their documents are being translated with the assistance of AI technologies. This transparency is not just a matter of professional ethics; it also affects the perception and trust of clients in the translation service. Transparency can be maintained by disclosing the use of AI or MT to clients. Nevertheless, in public perception, AI is a highly contested concept (Fast & Horvitz, 2017), so the issue presents a significant challenge in the language service industry.

The challenge surrounding transparency intertwines with the intricacies of intellectual property, particularly evident in the field of AI-generated translations. The issue of property rights raises significant concerns regarding the ownership of translations produced by artificial intelligence. Similarly, there is a need for reconsideration of authorship attribution to generative AI tools (Flanagin et al., 2023). As signalled by Tang et al. (2024: 315), "generative AI tools are nonlegal entities and are incapable of accepting responsibility and accountability for the content within the manuscript". The authors bring to the forefront a fundamental aspect of AI operation, which inherently lacks the capacity for moral judgement and legal accountability. In this case, ensuring that ethical standards and accountability are maintained may involve the development of new legal paradigms or the adaptation of existing ones to address the gap in accountability posed by the use of generative AI tools in translation.

Finally, a pivotal ethical issue pertains to preserving the translator's autonomy in environments augmented by AI. Although AI tools can enhance translators' capabilities, it is crucial to ensure that human translators continue to lead the decision-making process. If translators turn over their translating capacities to machines, they become less experienced at thus become gradually worse at this skill. The phenomenon of deskilling, as explored by Almer (2022), represents a significant consequence of the adoption of AI technologies. This process involves the diminution of both the requirement for specialised skills among workers, but also the ability to actually perform the task in question. The implications of deskilling can be profound, affecting not only the labour market, but also the way in which professional competencies are valued and developed. As AI continues to advance, the challenge becomes not only managing its integration into various sectors but also addressing the broader socio-economic impacts of this technological evolution on workforce skill requirements.

These ethical considerations underscore the necessity for revising the translator training curriculum, highlighting the potential implications for both the moral code and integrity of translation service provision, as well as the traditional translation skills (see Chapter 3). The shift towards AI systems undertaking translation tasks that previously necessitated translator expertise requires a careful balance between harnessing AI for improved efficiency and upholding the translator's unique expertise and essential autonomy. A selection of strategies through which translation trainees can foster retaining their autonomy and role within the translation process are discussed in Chapter 5, where the focus is laid on developing personal resources, even amidst the adoption and integration of AI technologies.

References

AI HLEG (High-Level Expert Group on Artificial Intelligence). 2019. 'Ethics Guidelines for Trustworthy AI'. The European Commission. https://ec.eur opa.eu/digital-single-market/en/news/ethics-guidelines-trustworthy-ai.

Alicea, Bradly. 2018. 'An Integrative Introduction to Human Augmentation Science'. *arXiv*. https://doi.org/10.48550/arXiv.1804.10521.

Almer, Jasmine. 2022. 'Deskilling as an Effect of AI: A Group of Students' Attitudes Towards AI and Their Worries About Deskilling'. Uppsala University. https://urn.kb.se/resolve?urn=urn:nbn:se:uu:diva-480935.

Bammel, Steven, dir. 2023. *Generative AI Iterative Translation*. https://vimeo.com/896464327.

Bird, Eleanor, Jasmin Fox-Skelly, Nicola Jenner, Ruth Larbey, Emma Weitkamp, and Alan Winfield. 2020. *The Ethics of Artificial Intelligence: Issues and Initiatives*. Brussels: European Parliamentary Research Service.

Bowker, Lynne, and Jairo Buitrago Ciro. 2019. 'Machine Translation and Global Research: Towards Improved Machine Translation Literacy in the Scholarly Community'. Emerald Publishing. https://doi.org/10.1108/9781787567214.

Canfora, Carmen, and Angelika Ottmann. 2020. 'Risks in Neural Machine Translation'. *Translation Spaces* 9 (1): 58–77. https://doi.org/10.1075/ts.00021.can.

Carl, Michael. 2020. 'Translation, Artificial Intelligence and Cognition'. In *The Routledge Handbook of Translation and Cognition*, 500–16. Routledge.

DePalma, Donald A. 2014. 'Free Machine Translation Can Leak Data'. *Tcworld Magazine* 2014. www.tcworld.info/e-magazine/translation-and-localization/free-machine-translation-can-leak-data-516/.

———. 2017. 'Augmented Translation Powers up Language Services'. *CSA Research*. 15 February 2017. https://csa-research.com/.

Dijk, Jan van. 2012. *The Network Society*. 3rd edition. London: Sage.
Drugan, Joanna. 2017. 'Ethics and Social Responsibility in Practice: Interpreters and Translators Engaging with and Beyond the Professions'. *The Translator* 23 (2): 126–42. https://doi.org/10.1080/13556509.2017.1281204.
Ehrensberger-Dow, Maureen, Alice Delorme Benites, and Caroline Lehr. 2023. 'A New Role for Translators and Trainers: Mt Literacy Consultants'. *Interpreter and Translator Trainer* 17 (3): 393–411. https://doi.org/10.1080/1750399X.2023.2237328.
Engelbart, Douglas C. 1962. 'Augmenting Human Intellect: A Conceptual Framework'. *SRI Summary Report AFOSR-3223*. www.dougengelbart.org/content/view/138/.
Fast, Ethan, and Eric Horvitz. 2017. 'Long-Term Trends in the Public Perception of Artificial Intelligence'. *Proceedings of the AAAI Conference on Artificial Intelligence* 31 (1). https://doi.org/10.1609/aaai.v31i1.10635.
Flanagin, Annette, Kirsten Bibbins-Domingo, Michael Berkwits, and Stacy L. Christiansen. 2023. 'Nonhuman "Authors" and Implications for the Integrity of Scientific Publication and Medical Knowledge'. *JAMA* 329 (8): 637–39. https://doi.org/10.1001/jama.2023.1344.
Green, Brian P. 2020. 'Artificial Intelligence and Ethics: Sixteen Challenges and Opportunities'. Markkula Center for Applied Ethics at Santa Clara University. 18 August 2020. www.scu.edu/ethics/all-about-ethics/artificial-intelligence-and-ethics-sixteen-challenges-and-opportunities/.
Guerberof Arenas, Ana. 2013. 'What Do Professional Translators Think about Post-Editing?' *Journal of Specialised Translation*, 19: 75–95.
Guerberof-Arenas, Ana, and Joss Moorkens. 2023. 'Ethics and Machine Translation: The End User Perspective'. In *Towards Responsible Machine Translation: Ethical and Legal Considerations in Machine Translation*, edited by Helena Moniz and Carla Parra Escartín, 113–33. Springer Verlag.
Gurov, Andrey. 2023. 'Advances in Artificial Intelligence in the Field of Literary Translation'. SSRN Scholarly Paper. Rochester, NY. https://doi.org/10.2139/ssrn.4465129.
Haque, Md. Asraful, and Shuai Li. 2024. 'Exploring ChatGPT and Its Impact on Society'. *AI and Ethics*, February. https://doi.org/10.1007/s43681-024-00435-4.
Herbert, Sarah, Félix do Carmo, Joanna Gough, and Anu Carnegie-Brown. 2023. 'From Responsibilities to Responsibility: A Study of the Effects of Translation Workflow Automation'. *Journal of Specialised Translation* 40: 9–35.
Horváth, Ildikó. 2022. 'Ai in Interpreting: Ethical Considerations'. *Across Languages and Cultures* 23 (1): 1–13. https://doi.org/10.1556/084.2022.00108.
Hutchins, John, and Harold Somers. 1992. *An Introduction to Machine Translation*. Academic Press.

Jiménez-Crespo, Miguel A. 2023. 'Augmentation and Translation Crowdsourcing: Are Collaborative Translators' Minds Truly "Augmented"?' *Translation, Cognition & Behavior*. https://doi.org/10.1075/tcb.00079.jim.

Johnson. 2017. 'Why Translators Have the Blues. A Profession under Pressure'. *The Economist*, 24 May 2017. www.economist.com/news/books-and-arts/21722609-.

Kenny, Dorothy, Joss Moorkens, and Félix do Carmo. 2020. 'Fair Mt: Towards Ethical, Sustainable Machine Translation'. *Translation Spaces* 9 (August): 1. https://doi.org/10.1075/ts.00018.int.

Koehn, Philipp. 2009. *Statistical Machine Translation*. Cambridge: Cambridge University Press.

Krings, Hans P., and Geoffrey S. Koby. 2001. *Repairing Texts: Empirical Investigations of Machine Translation Post-Editing Processes*. Kent, OH: Kent State University Press.

Larsson, Stefan, Mikael Anneroth, Anna Felländer, Li Felländer-Tsai, Fredrik Heintz, and Rebecka Cedering Ångström. 2019. *Sustainable AI: An Inventory of the State of Knowledge of Ethical, Social, and Legal Challenges Related to Artificial Intelligence*. AI Sustainability Center. https://aisustainability.org/publications/hallbar-ai-sustainable-ai/.

Lommel, Arle. 2020. 'Augmented Translation: Are We There Yet?' CSA Research. 4 November 2020. https://csa-research.com/Blogs-Events/Blog/augmented-translation-2020.

Lumeras, Maite Aragonés, and Andy Way. 2017. 'On the Complementarity Between Human Translators and Machine Translation'. *HERMES – Journal of Language and Communication in Business*, 56 (October): 21–42. https://doi.org/10.7146/hjlcb.v0i56.97200.

Martin, Sergio, Gabriel Diaz, Elio Sancristobal, Rosario Gil, Manuel Castro, and Juan Peire. 2011. 'New Technology Trends in Education: Seven Years of Forecasts and Convergence'. *Computers & Education* 57 (3): 1893–1906. https://doi.org/10.1016/j.compedu.2011.04.003.

McDonough, Julie. 2007. 'How Do Language Professionals Organize Themselves? An Overview of Translation Networks'. *Meta: Translators' Journal* 52 (4): 793–815.

Moorkens, Joss, and Sharon O'Brien. 2017. 'Assessing User Interface Needs of Post-Editors of Machine Translation'. In *Human Issues in Translation Technology*, edited by Dorothy Kenny, 109–30. Abingdon: Routledge.

Mossop, Brian. 2006. 'Has Computerization Changed Translation?' *Meta* 51 (4): 787–805.

O'Brien, Sharon. 2007. 'An Empirical Investigation of Temporal and Technical Post-Editing Effort'. *Translation and Interpreting Studies* 2 (1): 83–136.

———. 2012. 'Translation as Human–Computer Interaction'. *Translation Spaces* 1 (1): 101–22. https://doi.org/10.1075/ts.1.05obr.

———. 2023. 'Human-Centered Augmented Translation: Against Antagonistic Dualisms'. *Perspectives*, 1–16. https://doi.org/10.1080/09076 76X.2023.2247423.

O'Brien, Sharon, and Alessandra Rossetti. 2020. 'Neural Machine Translation and the Evolution of the Localisation Sector: Implications for Training'. *Journal of Internationalization and Localization* 7 (1–2): 95–221. https://doi.org/10.1075/jial.20005.obr.

Raisamo, Roope, Ismo Rakkolainen, Päivi Majaranta, Katri Salminen, Jussi Rantala, and Ahmed Farooq. 2019. 'Human Augmentation: Past, Present and Future'. *50 Years of the International Journal of Human-Computer Studies.* Reflections on the Past, Present and Future of Human-Centred Technologies 131 (November): 131–43. https://doi.org/10.1016/j.ijhcs.2019.05.008.

Risku, Hanna, Jelena Milosevic, and Regina Rogl. 2021. 'Responsibility, Powerlessness and Conflict: An Ethnographic Case Study of Boundary Management in Translation'. In *Translating Asymmetry – Rewriting Power*, edited by Ovidi Carbonell, Cortés and Esther Monzó-Nebot 145–68. John Benjamins. https://ucris.univie.ac.at/portal/en/publications/res ponsibility-powerlessness-and-conflict-an-ethnographic-case-study-of-boundary-management-in-translation(32b76877-480e-4c57-aac8-e64d8 5d5fd62).html.

Salmi, Hannu, Helena Thuneberg, and Mari-Pauliina Vainikainen. 2017. 'Making the Invisible Observable by Augmented Reality in Informal Science Education Context'. *International Journal of Science Education, Part B* 7 (3): 253–68.

Schäffner, Christina. 2020. 'Translator's Roles and Responsibilities'. In *The Bloomsbury Companion to Language Industry Studies*, edited by Erik Angelone, Maureen Ehrensberger-Dow, and Gary Massey, 63–89. London: Bloomsbury.

Stanney, Kay, Brent Winslow, Kelly Hale, and Dylan Schmorrow. 2015. 'Augmented Cognition'. In *APA Handbook of Human Systems Integration*, edited by Deborah A. Boehm-Davis, Francis T. Durso, and John D. Lee, 329–43. American Psychological Association. https://doi.org/10.1037/14528-021.

Sutskever, Ilya, Oriol Vinyals, and Quoc V. Le. 2014. 'Sequence to Sequence Learning with Neural Networks'. *arXiv*. https://doi.org/10.48550/arXiv.1409.3215.

Tang, Arthur, Kin-Kit Li, Kin On Kwok, Liujiao Cao, Stanley Luong, and Wilson Tam. 2024. 'The Importance of Transparency: Declaring the Use of Generative Artificial Intelligence (Ai) in Academic Writing'. *Journal of Nursing Scholarship* 56 (2): 314–18. https://doi.org/10.1111/jnu.12938.

Tomarenko, Valerij. 2019. *Through the Client's Eyes: How to Make Your Translations Visible*. Berlin BDÜ Fachverlag.

Vaswani, Ashish, Noam Shazeer, Niki Parmar, Jakob Uszkoreit, Llion Jones, Aidan N. Gomez, Lukasz Kaiser, and Illia Polosukhin. 2023. 'Attention Is All You Need'. *arXiv*. https://doi.org/10.48550/arXiv.1706.03762.

Vieira, Lucas Nunes, Carol O'Sullivan, Xiaochun Zhang, and Minako O'Hagan. 2023. 'Privacy and Everyday Users of Machine Translation'. *Translation Spaces* 12 (1): 21–44. https://doi.org/10.1075/ts.22012.nun.

Weber, Michael. 2018. 'AI in Translation: Future Role of Human Translators'. *TCLoc Master's* (blog). 2 October 2018. https://mastertcloc.unistra.fr/2018/10/02/artificial-intelligence-human-translators/.

Wu, Tongshuang, Michael Terry, and Carrie Jun Cai. 2022. 'AI Chains: Transparent and Controllable Human-AI Interaction by Chaining Large Language Model Prompts'. In *Proceedings of the 2022 CHI Conference on Human Factors in Computing Systems*, 1–22. New York, NY: Association for Computing Machinery. https://doi.org/10.1145/3491102.3517582.

Zhu, Minghai. 2023. 'Sustainability of Translator Training in Higher Education'. *PLOS One* 18 (5). https://doi.org/10.1371/journal.pone.0283522.

3 Translators as AI-assisted language specialists

3.1 Translators' new roles and status

All these AI technologies have led to a paradigm shift in translation services, essentially transforming translators into AI-assisted language specialists. This transition is not merely a change in the toolset, but signifies a deeper evolution in the role and expertise of translators. Traditionally, translators have been viewed as communication experts who mediate between languages and cultures (e.g. Nida, 1964; Newmark, 1988; Gouadec, 2007; Kinnunen & Koskinen, 2010; Schäffner 2020); with AI's integration, their role can be seen as either expanding or diminishing.

First, the diminishing role of the translator has been signalled by scholars such as Pym (2004), who observes "a narrowing of the role of translation, and thus an overlooking of the knowledge and advice that translators might be able to contribute" (2004: 164). Indeed, this concerning trend – where the diverse competencies and insights of translators are marginalised – emphasises the necessity of re-evaluating the roles and contributions translators can offer in the broader context of communication and cultural exchange. Given that automation is changing the translation profession not only in aspects related to the translation process but also in other translation services like managing translation projects (see Herbert et al., 2023), it remains evident that market segmentation within the translation industry is a prevailing reality.

Automation in translation leads to the fragmentation of translation tasks and specialties; translators are compelled to adapt by specialising in niche areas where their expertise and human touch remain indispensable, thus navigating the changing dynamics of the profession.

DOI: 10.4324/9781003521822-4

Vieira (2020: online) cautions against abandoning technical domains in response to automation threats, arguing that "any approach to automation threats that involves abandoning technical domains is likely to reinforce these market segmentation effects". Concentrating translators' efforts away from technical domains, where automation is most prevalent, may lead to marginalising certain areas of translation work and entrenching the divide between automated and human-centric translation tasks. Such a shift, while potentially safeguarding certain aspects of the translator's role and status, might inadvertently solidify the segmentation and divisions within the market, potentially also limiting translators' opportunities and the diversity of their skill sets.

Vieira (ibid.) further notes that while branding services separately may appear unavoidable, "hierarchising them could ultimately be a missed opportunity for keeping all these services closely knit under the aegis of translators". This insight suggests the need for a paradigm shift in both individual translators' and the broader industry's strategies, that is, a reconsideration of how translators and the industry as a whole approach the challenge of automation. It advocates for a more integrated, holistic strategy that preserves the translator's involvement across a broader spectrum of domains, thus preserving their relevance and adaptability in an increasingly automated landscape.

It is hoped that the transition from conventional translation methodologies to a more collaborative interaction with AI does not inherently imply a diminished role for the translator. Instead, translators can be viewed from a perspective where they serve as facilitators who enrich AI outputs, rather than merely utilising them. This conceptualisation of translators as intermediaries who enhance AI outputs underscores the value added by human expertise in refining and elevating the quality of machine-generated translations.

The expanding role can, therefore, be seen as the indispensable role of a safeguard. It expands to include the management of AI tools. Therefore, the translator operating within hybrid translation workflows assumes roles that include, but are not limited to, the following:

- **editorial oversight**: supervising the output of AI-assisted translation, ensuring the preservation of meaning, linguistic subtleties, cultural contexts, diverse forms of humour, metaphors and other elements that embody the essence and value of the source text;
- **quality assurance**: guaranteeing the accuracy, coherence, consistency, logical flow and readability of the target text;

Translators as AI-assisted language specialists 53

- **cultural consultant**: providing insights into cultural sensitivities, regional discrepancies, national associations or ambiguous expressions to ensure linguistic accuracy but also cultural congruence;
- **technology liaison**: using the software, customising its settings, managing the process of AI assistance in translation;
- **ethical safeguard**: upholding ethical standards within the AI-assisted translation process, ensuring that the target text is reliable, faithful and devoid of biases or any misinformation.

All these new tasks require a deep understanding of both the source and target languages, as well as the ability to discern and correct errors that automated systems may overlook. What is crucial to emphasise here is that AI-generated texts tend to look impeccable and seemingly coherent, but a reasonable and ethical use of AI-assisted translation involves rigorous proofreading, editing, and retranslation to meet the highest standards of quality.

In hybrid translation workflows, the translator acts as a final checkpoint before translated materials reach their intended audience, which may involve functioning as editors and managers to ensure the required standards of quality and fidelity. Although seemingly less human involvement is necessary in hybrid workflows, human intuition and vigilance become more critical than ever before as translators balance the efficiency of automation with the need for ethical responsibility.

Furthermore, the new roles of translators in hybrid translation workflows necessitate a re-evaluation of translator training. Academic institutions and professional training programs must consider adapting their curricula to include technical training in AI tools (see Chapter 5). This integration seems essential for preparing future translators to serve as AI-assisted language specialists with the necessary skills to thrive in this increasingly automated industry. Apart from technical skills, with such technological advancements, translators must continuously adapt to stay competent and relevant in their profession. The following sections aim to provide an overview of the areas of translation expertise where special attention is required for translators to remain competitive.

3.2 Future translator expertise: what is missing?

With the rise of augmented translation and hybrid workflows, defining the requisite skill set for an individual to be recognised as a translator has become more challenging than ever before. It has been acknowledged that translation expertise necessitates a blend of competencies (see Kelly 2005, 2007; Gouadec 2007; Göpferich 2009; Tiselius & Hild 2017; Doherty, 2018; Risku & Schlager, 2022). The concept has been characterised using two terms of "virtual identity in usage" (Shreve et al., 2018: 49) – that is competence and expertise – with more inclination towards the term expertise within cognitive-psychological approaches. Translation expertise includes such capabilities as linguistic proficiency, translation competence, technical skills also known as strategic or instrumental competence and attitudinal or psycho-physiological disposition (see PACTE, 2003, 2008; EMT, 2009, 2017).

The technical competencies of translators have consistently been held in high regard and sought after in the field. Torrejón and Rico (2013) highlight an increasing requirement for specialised expertise in the post-editing of machine-translated content, underscoring the evolving translation demands. Since the work of the AI-assisted translator closely resembles that of a machine translation (MT) post-editor, let us reconsider translation competence from the perspective of integrating technological fluency and adaptive strategies into the core skill set. Torrejón and Rico (ibid.) explore the profile of translators working as MT post-editors and define their competences, arguing that post-translation editing skills are mainly divided into three aspects: core competencies, linguistic skills and instrumental competence. Core competence involves a combination of psycho-physiological skills, including a refined understanding and personal management of post-translational editing conventions, an attentive consideration of client expectations and adeptness in handling uncertainties. Additionally, it encompasses the strategic insight essential for effective editing and revision processes, aimed at achieving coherence and resonance with the intended message and the cultural and linguistic preferences of the target audience. This set of competencies underscores the complex nature of translation services, highlighting the importance of both technical proficiency and adaptive strategies in professional practice.

The skillset necessary for translators to stay afloat in an increasingly automated industry is, however, not limited to technical or instrumental competences, but includes the psychological capital of the translator which can have an impact on how successful they are in pursuing a career in language industry (see Atkinson, 2012; Pietrzak, 2022). Angelone (2023) advocates for a stronger focus on adaptive expertise in translation and translator training to enable optimal performance in today's language industry. Adaptive expertise is dependent on the psychological capital of the translator, which encompasses a variety of components, including self-efficacy and self-regulation, which collectively contribute to a translator's ability to face challenges, adapt to changing demands and seize opportunities within the dynamic field of language services (see Pietrzak, 2022).

The relationship between personal resources and translator expertise has been explored in a more in-depth manner, with a growing interest in understanding how individual differences affect translation expertise, for instance by Jääskeläinen (2012), Lacruz and Jääskeläinen (2018), Muñoz Martín (2010, 2013, 2014), Muñoz Martín & Olalla-Soler (2022), Klimkowski (2015, 2019), Núñez and Bolaños-Medina (2018) or Saldanha & O'Brien (2013). Hubscher-Davison (2009, 2013, 2016, 2017, 2020). Hubscher-Davison's comprehensive investigation into translators' personalities (2013) shows the psychological dimensions underpinning translation competence with the role of intuition and emotional intelligence in facing the complexities of cross-linguistic and cross-cultural communication. This evolving discourse on translator competence underscores the necessity of integrating psychological perspectives into translator training and professional development to enhance both individual and industry-wide success.

Sections 3.3–3.6 discuss various aspects of translator competence, from technical skills to personal resources – encompassing metacognitive and psychological dimensions – which all require cultivation to enable digital resilience and adaptability to the new hybrid translation workflows.

3.3 Technical skills for hybrid workflows

The collaboration between human translators and AI has the potential to enhance translation processes and results. However, it requires a comprehensive understanding of how AI functions and how it can be integrated into the translation workflow. It is, therefore, important for translators to develop expertise in using translation tools and platforms that are driven by AI. This includes understanding how NMT systems, translation memory software, and AI-powered tools work to help with the translation process. They need to develop technical proficiency, which involves troubleshooting common problems (losing connection with GenAI API, for example) and making the most out of technology to improve accuracy and efficiency.

Depending on the workflow, the translation process can start with a human prompt. Regardless of the starting point, the core process of the collaboration involves the initial heavy lifting of translating large volumes of text by the AI. Following this, human translators refine these AI-generated translations, focusing on aspects that require human insight, such as idiomatic expressions, cultural sensitivity and stylistic preferences. To effectively utilise and interact with constantly improving technologies, translators must cultivate a range of data literacy skills (see Krüger, 2022). A foundational understanding of AI and machine learning principles is crucial (Bammel, 2023), particularly how these technologies apply to natural language processing and machine translation. This knowledge enables translators to grasp the capabilities and limitations of AI tools, facilitating more informed use and integration into their workflows. Skills like data management and curation or AI prompting may soon become on par with translation expertise. AI systems, especially in translation, heavily depend on the quality of the data they are trained on. Translators must be adept at collecting, organising and curating relevant data sets to improve NMT (European Union, 2019) and AI performance (see GAIT workflow in Section 2.1.2, for example).

Pre-editing is yet another set of skills that requires redefinition in the context of AI-powered translation. Pre-editing for MT, particularly for NMT systems, "involves rewriting parts of source texts in a way that is supposed to ensure better quality outputs when those texts are translated by machine" (Sánchez-Gijón & Kenny, 2022: 81). This often includes (Bowker, 2002; Guerberof Arenas, 2019; Miyata & Fujita, 2021):

- simplifying complex sentence structures to make them more amenable to MT;
- standardising terminology and spelling to match the training data of the MT system;
- removing or clarifying ambiguities and idiomatic expressions that MT systems may not handle well;
- ensuring consistency in style and terminology to improve the coherence of the translated text;
- These modifications are aimed at reducing the cognitive load on the MT system, minimising errors in translation that stem from

linguistic complexity or nuances not well-represented in the system's training data.

However pre-editing is a process of preparing source texts predominantly for translation using NMT systems, it also applies to GenAI translations. Despite their shared goal of optimising translation quality, the approaches and considerations can differ significantly due to the underlying technology and its capabilities. The primary difference lies in the nature of the systems' limitations and strengths. Pre-editing for MT systems is mainly about simplification and clarification to avoid mistranslation. In contrast, pre-editing for GenAI involves strategically guiding the system to use its creative and generative capabilities effectively while maintaining accuracy and adherence to the source text.

While fluency and creativity of output are strengths of GenAI, ensuring accuracy and faithfulness to the source becomes paramount. In this case, pre-editing does not apply to the document as such. It is instead focused on the effective prompting of the GenAI system in order to achieve the expected results (see Lester et al., 2021; Reynolds & McDonell, 2021):

- clearly defining the purpose and expected outcome of the translation to align with the capabilities of GenAI;
- crafting prompts or instructions that guide the AI in generating translations that meet specific stylistic or tonal requirements;
- providing contextual or background information within prompts to improve the relevance and accuracy of the AI-generated text;
- adjusting the source text to prevent the GenAI from introducing unwarranted creativity or straying too far from the original meaning;
- loop-feeding revised bit of translation to improve translation quality;
- The focus in GenAI-based workflows is on leveraging the model's strengths while guarding against its propensity to generate content that, while fluent, may not accurately reflect the source text's intent.

The quality of the AI output largely depends on the quality of the instruction that is given (Peng et al., 2023). Translators, who are trained language specialists by default, may seize the opportunity and learn how to prompt AI to generate the desired output effectively. As was already mentioned, prompting involves crafting questions or commands in a way that guides the AI to produce translations of expected quality or other data expected by the translator. This skill is crucial for leveraging GenAI's capabilities in creative translation tasks, such as generating multiple translation options, suggesting idiomatic expressions or even providing cultural context insights (see Section 2.2 for more information).

The rise of NMT and AI in translation has led to an increased need for post-editing, where human translators refine and correct NMT- and AI-generated translations. Translators must hone their post-editing skills, focusing on efficiency and improving the quality of machine output to meet human standards (Doherty, 2018). While the EMT framework (2012, online) lists MT post editing under translation competence – that is, "students know how to … (p)ost-edit MT output using style guides and terminology glossaries to maintain quality standards in MT-enhanced translation projects" – it does not mention AI post-editing, which, while similar, requires a different approach from the translator.

While in the case of MT the focus of the post-editor is typically on (see Krings, 2001; O'Brien, 2002; Torrejón & Rico, 2013; Koponen, 2016; Guerberof Arenas, 2019; Nitzke & Hansen-Schirra, 2021):

- correcting grammatical errors and ensuring syntactic accuracy;
- ensuring that the translated text adheres to terminological consistency, especially in technical or specialised texts;
- improving the readability and fluency of the text to match human translation standards;
- ensuring that the translation is faithful to the source text in terms of meaning and intent;
- MT systems, particularly NMT, have become highly proficient in producing translations that are syntactically coherent and increasingly accurate in terms of semantics. However, they may still struggle with context, idiomatic expressions, and cultural nuances, requiring human intervention to achieve the desired level of quality and appropriateness.

GenAI, particularly when involving LLMs like GPT, introduces a different set of challenges and considerations when it comes to post-editing. The primary distinction lies in the nature of errors and the focus of the post-editing process. MT-translation post-editing often focuses on correcting errors stemming from the system's inability to fully grasp complex language patterns, nuances, and context (Briva-Iglesias et al., 2023). In contrast, GenAI-translation post-editing might deal more with issues related to over-generation, inaccuracies, or deviations from the source content due to the model's creativity and its potential to introduce new content not present in the original text (Ji et al., 2023; Lee, 2023; Peng et al., 2023), as discussed below:

- GenAI models can produce highly fluent text that mimics human writing styles closely. However, they may fabricate content (hallucinate, see Guerreiro et al., 2023), or stray from the source text's intended meaning (Ji et al., 2022; Guerreiro et al., 2023), requiring careful verification of accuracy and fidelity.
- These systems can generate creative and idiomatic expressions that fit well within the target language's cultural context. However, ensuring these creative liberties still accurately represent the source text's information is crucial (Köbis & Mossink, 2021).
- Prompting plays a significant role in the output of GenAI translations. The effectiveness of post-editing may also involve refining prompts to achieve better initial outputs (Wu et al., 2022; Peng et al., 2023).
- Since GenAI can incorporate broader context and generate text with a high degree of fluency, post-editing may also involve assessing the appropriateness of the generated text (Lee, 2023) within a wider discourse or narrative context, which is especially relevant for literary or nuanced texts.

To sum up, the skills required for effective post-editing may differ. Post-editing MT translations may demand a strong understanding of the source and target languages and expertise in the domain of the text (Torrejón & Rico, 2013). GenAI translations require critical thinking and creativity to accurately translate nuanced and culturally sensitive content (Guerberof Arenas & Toral, 2020). Human translators' understanding of context, idiomatic expressions, and cultural nuances remains irreplaceable despite AI advancements. When working with AI, translators must use these skills to complement AI-generated translations for the intended audience.

The field of AI-powered translation is rapidly evolving, necessitating a commitment from all language specialists to continuous learning and adaptability (Tiselius & Hild, 2017; Angelone & Marín García, 2019; Pokrivcakova, 2019; Muñoz-Basols et al., 2023; Škobo & Petričević, 2023). Since translation expertise involves "maximal adaptation to task constraints" (Muñoz Martín, 2014: 10), staying informed about the latest technological advancements and adapting to new workflows is crucial for translators to remain competitive and effective. The implications for translator education presented in Chapter 5, continuous skill development and fostering personal resources seem essential in the evolving AI-assisted translation, especially considering the current stage of AI development and predictions for the future (see Section 1.3).

3.4 From anxiety to digital resilience

Technological advancements, while designed to enhance productivity and efficiency, can introduce challenges that negatively impact translators' work environments and the overall quality of their output (see Section 2.3). Studies have highlighted a growing dissatisfaction resulting from not only mere technologies but also the resulting business practices (LeBlanc, 2017; Cadwell et al., 2018). There has been an increasing concern among translators towards the compulsory adoption of technologies dictated by clients (see Alonso & Vieira, 2017; Vieira, 2020; Pietrzak & Kornacki, 2021). It is an issue compounded by what is perceived as insufficient compensation for specific tasks, particularly in post-editing work (Guerberof Arenas, 2013; Guerberof Arenas & Moorkens, 2023).

This dissatisfaction is further exacerbated by organisational and ergonomic studies which emphasise the constraints technology places on translators, affecting their creative expression and independence in their profession (Ehrensberger-Dow & Massey, 2014; Massey & Ehrensberger-Dow, 2017). Research conducted by Olohan (2015) and further investigations into the ergonomics of translation work environments (Ehrensberger-Dow & Massey, 2013, 2014, 2017) have shed light on the ambivalence translators feel towards technology. While technology is integral to modern translation practices, its arbitrary imposition by external parties can lead to a sense of alienation and discontent among translators. This imposition often forces translators to conform to technological frameworks that may not align with their personal work strategies, leading to a perceived devaluation of their skills and undermining their professional autonomy (see also Sections 2.3 and 2.4).

Cognitive and ergonomic research into translation processes (Ehrensberger-Dow & Massey, 2013, 2014, Muñoz Martín & González Fernández 2021) reveals significant insights into how the application of technological tools influences translators' work habits and mental states. The constraints imposed by technology not only limit translators' creative capabilities but also affect their sense of control over their work, leading to different forms of technology-induced anxiety. Walczyński (2021: 100) identifies anxiety as a significant negative psycho-affective factor in translation and interpreting, manifesting either as archaic anxiety, which stems from past events and experiences, or as existential anxiety, which pertains to present and future situations. While most aspects of anxiety within translation workflows are predominantly related to current circumstances, some of them, for instance automation anxiety, can also stem from former preconceptions and beliefs, for example, about the nature of the profession or translators' roles and status (see Section 3.1).

A specific type of anxiety experienced in the context of using translation technology is referred to as cognitive friction (O'Brien et al., 2017). This phenomenon typically arises from unforeseen circumstances encountered during the translation process, leading to a sense of mental strain or discomfort as translators navigate these unexpected challenges. According to O'Brien et al. (2017: 147), cognitive friction arises from the unnecessary cognitive burden that results from counterproductive CAT tools features.

Another type of anxiety related to the use of technological tools in translation can stem from the constant pressure to adapt to new tools and processes, presenting a persistent challenge as translators strive to keep pace with the rapid evolution of technology. As signalled by Pietrzak and Kornacki (2021: 61), technological anxiety is typically caused by unfamiliarity with specific technological tools available. Translators suffering from this anxiety doubt their capability to effectively manage issues related to the use of computers. It manifests a fear of embracing new tech-related tasks, identifying strategies to confront these challenges and integrating acquired skills in the future. This complex relationship between translators and technology underscores the need for a more nuanced understanding of technological integration in the translation industry and translator training, ensuring that it serves to empower rather than constrain professional translators.

Yet another dimension of technology-induced anxiety, arising from the integration of technological tools into translation, has come to be known as automation anxiety. Automation invariably generates new demands within a profession, often leading to the creation of new roles and responsibilities (see Section 3.1) and the necessity for skill adaptation (see Section 3.2). The extent of automation can differ significantly across various professions. This extent, or degree of automation, is defined as the proportion of functions executed automatically compared to the total number of functions within a profession (Nof, 2009). It needs to be stressed that automation does indeed substitute for labour, but it also complements labour (Autor, 2015).

Wiener's (1989) discussion of the concept of automation in the context of technological advancements in aviation emphasises that the effect of automation on workload is not uniform. Wiener's (ibid.) concept of "clumsy automation" highlights the varied impact of automation on workload. A similar perspective can be applied to the field of translation, where automation not only uniformly reduces workload but also redistributes tasks and responsibilities over time. This redistribution may involve shifting the translator's focus from routine, repetitive tasks to more complex tasks or from translating to post-editing. As observed by Herbert et al. (2023: 9), "automation can both restrict and enhance professional roles and autonomy", but it definitely redefines the translator's role (see Section 3.1), emphasising the need for adaptability and the development of skills that are either beyond AI capabilities or that become necessary due to the changes brought about by automation.

This phenomenon of automation encapsulates the apprehension felt by professional translators in response to the increasing automation of translation processes, reflecting concerns about the potential displacement of human translators by AI systems and the consequent impact on employment dynamics within the industry (see Pym & Torres-Simón, 2021). Automation threatens to leave certain workers behind; as highlighted by Brynjolfsson and McAfee (2014: 11), "there's never been a worse time to be a worker with only 'ordinary' skills and abilities to offer, because computers, robots, and other digital technologies are acquiring these skills and abilities at an extraordinary rate". Some translators may indeed find themselves increasingly marginalised; thus, the move towards automation emphasises the need for changes in how we approach translator education.

It is crucial to focus on fostering future translators' skills, adaptability and digital resilience, to prepare them for the changing translation industry and ensure they can compete in an economy increasingly dominated by technology. Digital resilience is defined as the ability to adapt to various tasks and environments (Garista & Pocett, 2014). This concept encompasses the capability to adapt, recover and thrive amid technological changes. Resilience can be understood as a "manifested competence in the context of significant challenges to adaptation or development" (Masten & Coatsworth, 1998: 207). The concept can be defined simultaneously as the ability to recover rapidly from difficult situations as well as the capacity to endure ongoing hardship in every conceivable way (Walker et al., 2006: 251).

In educational settings, learner resilience is recognised as a crucial factor that contributes to effective learning and successful study outcomes in higher education (Walker et al., 2006; Holdsworth et al., 2018). In hybrid translation workflows, it is built on recognising risks, mastering effective strategies, learning from experience and securing reliable support. It refers to translators' ability to effectively manage risks associated with the use of technology in their work, which involves applying effective strategies to deal with them, learning from past experiences to improve future practices and having access to appropriate support when needed.

Digital resilience in translators is a metacognitive capacity that enhances and complements translator competence. It can be seen as a manifestation of the translator's self-regulation in the digital context. Digital resilience involves not only the technical skills to use computer tools but also the mindset to embrace technological changes as opportunities for efficiency and growth. The translator's openness to new digital solutions not only influences their interaction with technology but also enhances their ability to recognise how these technologies can innovate and transform individual workflows.

An approach to translators' technological anxiety advised by Vieira (2020) involves "open dialogue among translation industry stakeholders and the exploration of business models that integrate rather than fragment the role of translators across domains" (2020: 21). By advocating for integration rather than fragmentation, Vieira highlights the importance of viewing translators as vital components of the translation process, whose roles can evolve with technology rather than be replaced by it. This approach not only aims to reduce anxiety but also promotes a more sustainable and inclusive future for the translation industry, where technology enhances human capabilities rather than diminishing them.

The concept of resilience capability emphasises the role of contextual factors, organisational variables and managerial guidelines in defining the organisational routines that influence the specific forms taken by technological change (Lengnick-Hall & Beck, 2005). Therefore, by adopting Vieira's approach and fostering an environment of open communication and innovative business models, translators can potentially remain resilient and integral to the process, using technology to enhance their work instead of viewing it as a threat to their financial stability or professional integrity.

3.5 Personal resources and metacognitive capacity

This section highlights the importance of the translator's metacognitive capacity and the psychological capital that allows for adaptability and self-development in the face of rapid technological transformations in the translation industry. Due to the emergence of new technologies, "transferable soft skills are more essential than ever" (O'Brien and Rossetti, 2020: 95) because of the significant change both in the nature of work and in the translator's role (see Section 3.1). While AI technologies have enhanced efficiency and created new opportunities, they also render certain translator skills obsolete, thereby shifting the focus towards skills that cannot be easily automated or replicated by technological tools (see Section 2.3). This transition underscores the value of personal resources, such as metacognitive capacity and digital resilience that are characterised by their applicability across different job roles and industries.

Personal resources are defined as integral components of the translator's self, comprising essential skills and attributes, alongside social and psychological assets. Resource-based perspectives on human adaptation emphasise the interplay between social resources and the resilient self, centring on skills and personal traits as delineated by Hobfoll (2002), Hobfoll et al. (2003) and Hobfoll et al. (2018). Key resources that a given group possess can be seen as management resources which contribute to better functioning and implementing other resources to meet stressful demands (Thoits, 1994). In contemporary psychology, the most extensively researched resources pertain to aspects of control (see Skinner, 1996). The control-related concept that is seen as a key resource for translators is self-efficacy, initially related only to a specific challenge, but then held as a key ability to exercise successful influence over the environment and goal accomplishment as well as stress resistance in the face of challenges (Bandura, 1995).

Such key resources as self-efficacy, self-regulation or self-concept can be regarded as the psychological capital of the translator, which is crucial for meeting professional demands successfully, as reported in Pietrzak (2022). These resources fall within strategic competence defined as a metacognitive competence that orchestrates the execution and operational aspects of various sub-competences (Göpferich, 2009: 22). Metacognition (Shreve, 2006, 2009; Muñoz Martín and Olalla-Soler, 2022) is a central element that makes translators active agents of their processes. Bergen (2009: 236) clarifies the concept of metacognition in the context of strategic competence, emphasising tasks such as identifying translation obstacles, applying remedies and assessing results. Atkinson and Crezee (2014) underscore the significance of metacognitive skills and personal resources, including self-motivation, self-efficacy and self-confidence, particularly in the context of freelance translation and interpreting. Metacognitive components of translator competence facilitate the execution of a translation task or the adjustment thereof, enabling performance. Metacognitive translator competence can, therefore, be defined as "the ability to self-regulate cognitive processes involved in translation, based on a set of personal resources that make up the psychological capital of the translator" (Pietrzak 2022: 16). The psychological capital of the translator equips the translator with the resilience and adaptability required in their profession, particularly as rapid advancements in AI technologies demand a strong metacognitive capacity to ensure competitiveness and success in the market.

The increasing importance of transferable metacognitive capacity necessitates a re-evaluation of current educational curricula and training programs to ensure that they are not solely focused on imparting technical knowledge but also on developing the metacognitive capacity that will be crucial for success in the future workplace (Shreve, 2009; Muñoz Martín, 2014; Pietrzak, 2022). This shift requires a holistic approach to education and training, one that integrates metacognitive capacity development into various learning experiences and prepares individuals not just for the jobs of today but for the ability to adapt to the jobs of tomorrow.

Translation student personal resources that are especially important in interactions with AI technologies are self-efficacy (Atkinson, 2012; Haro-Soler, 2017, 2018, 2019), self-development or continuous self-directed learning (Shreve, 2009; Muñoz Martín, 2013; Pietrzak, 2022), self-regulation (Shreve, 2006, 2009; Muñoz Martín, 2014; Pietrzak, 2018; Haro Soler, 2021), self-reflection (Kußmaul, 1995; Hansen, 2006; Norberg, 2014), digital resilience and adaptive expertise (Angelone, 2023). It is crucial for young translators to embrace the concept of lifelong learning as a core component of their professional growth. This encompasses not only staying abreast of the latest advancements in translation technologies, but also recognising the significance of self-development and nurturing a positive self-concept. As the industry evolves, the ability to adapt and continuously refine one's skills becomes indispensable. Engaging with new tools and methodologies, while simultaneously investing in personal well-being and self-development, equips young translators with the digital resilience (see Section 3.4) and versatility needed to thrive in this constantly evolving professional environment. For more practical considerations, see Section 5.3 where the authors propose a set of guiding ideas aimed at fostering students' personal resources ensuring that translator training is not only adapted to the new AI-enhanced workflows but also prioritises the creation of safe and human-centric learning environments.

3.6 The translator's self-concept in AI interactions

The translator's self-concept encompasses a complex psychological construct, mirroring the diversity inherent in human self-perception. Originating from the early scholarly discussions by James (1890), self-concept has evolved to embody a construct that is as intricate as the varied lenses through which it is examined. Shavelson et al. (1976) define self-concept as a developmental and evaluative construct, shaped through experiences and interpretations of one's environment, further influenced by external reinforcements and evaluations. This hierarchy of self-concept spans from a general perception at the apex to more specific academic and non-academic components. The academic self-concept, for instance, encapsulates both descriptive and evaluative self-perceptions, crucial in educational and professional settings. Baumeister's (2011: 49) further explores the inherent complexity within self-concept by pointing out the myriad, often loosely connected beliefs that constitute individual self-concept. This intricate mesh of beliefs encompasses several dimensions of the self, including physical, mental, social, cognitive, automatic, working and the perceived self.

The interplay between self-concept and other self-constructs, such as self-efficacy, self-confidence and self-esteem, is of particular interest in understanding the translator's self-concept. While these constructs overlap, they hold distinct meanings and implications for subjective competence. Bong and Clark (1999) emphasise the complexity of self-concept, noting its cognitive and affective dimensions and its susceptibility to social comparison, in contrast to the more cognitively oriented self-efficacy. As observed by Muñoz Martín (2014), self-efficacy is an important element of translation expertise as it constitutes one of the minimal sub-dimensions of self-concept. The translator's self-concept can be defined as a confluence of self-beliefs and metacognitive processes which play a role in shaping translators' perceptions, competencies and educational paths, ultimately influencing their professional efficacy and professional identity.

The conceptualisation of the translator's self-concept as a bridge between the translator's social and psychological realms was explored by Kiraly (1990: 100), highlighting its role in shaping a sense of translation purposes, an awareness of the requirements of the translation task and self-evaluation. Kiraly's (2000) perspective on translator competence as a socially constructed, multifaceted skill set accentuates the importance of developing a nuanced translator's self-concept through education. This self-concept, perceived as self-competence, is descriptive and reflective of one's awareness and skills, serving as a manifestation of metacognition (see Pietrzak, 2022: 94). The relevance of self-concept in translation competence and education has been emphasised by scholars like Ehrensberger-Dow & Massey (2013), Muñoz Martín (2014), Haro Soler and Kiraly (2019) who underscore its impact on translators' understanding, handling of situations and coherent action. Within the spectrum of methodologies aimed at operationalising the translator's self-concept, Svahn (2016) delves into sociological perspectives that centre on the market dynamics, the translator's role and societal perceptions, offering valuable insights into this domain. Exploring the translator's self-concept reveals its operational challenges, yet it provides valuable insights into the metacognitive processes and self-development.

Metacognitive processes associated with self-concept, including self-regulation, self-monitoring and adaptability, play a vital role in managing the complexities of evolving environments and variable cognitive states (Shreve, 2009; Muñoz Martín, 2013). This interplay significantly emphasises the importance of an individual's capacity for introspective adjustment and recalibration amidst diverse and challenging conditions. In the current translation industry, the introduction of AI technologies and the adoption of hybrid workflows have significantly altered the traditional roles of translators. This new environment requires translators not only to possess linguistic skills but also to be proficient in technological tools, facilitating collaboration between human expertise and artificial intelligence.

In recent years, business practices in the translation industry have predominantly involved post-editing tasks and the utilisation of machine translation technologies (refer to LeBlanc, 2017; Cadwell et al, 2018; O'Brien & Rossetti, 2021). Currently, in the new, AI-assisted hybrid workflows, with the evolution in the role of translators (see Section 3.1), such a hybrid approach to translation needs to combine the strengths of both human translators and AI, emphasising the critical role of translators in enhancing the quality of machine-generated outputs through their deep understanding of language and culture. This technological shift has implications for the self-concept of translators within the industry. As interactions with AI become more frequent, translators must adapt their professional identity to encompass both linguistic expertise and technological competence.

This adaptation requires a commitment to ongoing professional development not only to keep pace with technological advancements in the field (Section 3.2), but also foster better metacognitive capacity (Section 3.4) to maintain the value and visibility of human expertise in a technology-driven market. Translators can position themselves as AI facilitators, quality controllers and editors of machine-generated translations, focusing on tasks that require cultural sensitivity, creativity or domain-specific knowledge that AI cannot replicate. This knowledge is indispensable to improve and authenticate AI-assisted translations so as to ensure that translations are not only linguistically accurate but also thoroughly resonant with the intended audience. A selection of practical ideas for facilitating metacognitive skills and translators' personal resources such as self-concept, self-efficacy and self-reflection are presented in Section 5.4.

References

Alonso, Elisa, and Lucas Nunes Vieira. 2017. 'The Translator's Amanuensis 2020'. *JoSTrans: The Journal of Specialised Translation*, no. 28 (July): 345–61.

Angelone, Erik. 2023. 'Weaving Adaptive Expertise into Translator Training'. In *The Human Translator in the 2020s*, edited by Gary Massey, Elisa Huertas Barros, and David Katan, 60–73. Routledge.

Angelone, Erik, and Álvaro Marín García. 2019. 'Gauging Perceptions and Behaviors of Translators and Project Managers: Expertise Acquisition Through Deliberate Practice'. In *Translation Practice in the Field: Current Research on Socio-Cognitive Processes*, edited by Hanna Risku, Regina Rogl, and Jelena Milosevic, 123–60. Benjamins Current Topics. John Benjamins Publishing Company. https://doi.org/10.1075/bct.105.07ang.

Atkinson, David. 2012. 'Freelance Translator Success and Psychological Skill: A Study of Translator Competence with Perspectives from Work Psychology'. Unpublished PhD thesis, New Zealand: The University of Auckland. https://researchspace.auckland.ac.nz/handle/2292/18723.

Atkinson, David, and Ineke Crezee. 2014. 'Improving Psychological Skill in Trainee Interpreters'. *International Journal of Interpreter Education* 6 (1): 3–18.

Autor, David H. 2015. 'Why Are There Still so Many Jobs? The History and Future of Workplace Automation'. *Journal of Economic Perspectives* 29 (3): 3–30. https://doi.org/10.1257/jep.29.3.3.

Bammel, Steven, dir. 2023. *Generative AI Iterative Translation*. https://vimeo.com/896464327.

Bandura, Albert. 1995. 'Exercise of Personal and Collective Efficacy in Changing Societies'. In *Self-Efficacy in Changing Societies*, edited by Albert Bandura, 1–45. Cambridge: Cambridge University Press. https://doi.org/10.1017/CBO9780511527692.003.

Baumeister, Roy F. 2011. 'Self and Identity: A Brief Overview of What They Are, What They Do, and How They Work'. *Annals of the New York Academy of Sciences* 1234 (1): 48–55. https://doi.org/10.1111/j.1749-6632.2011.06224.x.

Bergen, David. 2009. 'The Role of Metacognition and Cognitive Conflict in the Development of Translation Competence'. *Across Languages and Cultures* 10 (2): 231–50. https://doi.org/10.1556/Acr.10.2009.2.4.

Bong, Mimi, and Richard E. Clark. 1999. 'Comparison Between Self-Concept and Self-Efficacy in Academic Motivation Research'. *Educational Psychologist* 34 (3): 139–53. https://doi.org/10.1207/s15326985ep3403_1.

Bowker, Lynne. 2002. *Computer-Aided Translation Technology: A Practical Introduction*. University of Ottawa Press.

Briva-Iglesias, Vicent, Sharon O'Brien, and Benjamin R. Cowan. 2023. 'The Impact of Traditional and Interactive Post-Editing on Machine Translation User Experience, Quality, and Productivity'. *Translation, Cognition & Behavior* 6 (1): 60–86. https://doi.org/10.1075/tcb.00077.bri.

Brynjolfsson, Erik, and Andrew McAfee. 2014. *The Second Machine Age: Work, Progress, and Prosperity in a Time of Brilliant Technologies*.

The Second Machine Age: Work, Progress, and Prosperity in a Time of Brilliant Technologies. New York, NY, US: W W Norton & Co.

Cadwell, Patrick, Sharon O'Brien, and Carlos S. C. Teixeira. 2018. 'Resistance and Accommodation: Factors for the (Non-) Adoption of Machine Translation Among Professional Translators'. *Perspectives* 26 (3): 301–21. https://doi.org/10.1080/0907676X.2017.1337210.

Doherty, Stephen. 2018. 'The Impact of Translation Technologies on the Process and Product of Translation'. *International Journal of Communication* 12: 111–31.

Ehrensberger-Dow, Maureen, and Gary Massey. 2013. 'Indicators of Translation Competence: Translators' Self-Concepts and the Translation of Titles'. *Journal of Writing Research* 5 (1): 103–31. https://doi.org/10.17239/jowr-2013.05.01.5.

———. 2014. 'Constraints on Creativity: The Case of CAT Tools'. Innsbruck: University of Innsbruck..

EMT. 2009. 'Competences for Professional Translators, Experts in Multilingual and Multimedia Communication'. Brussels: European Commission.

———. 2017. 'EMT Competence Framework 2017'. 2017. https://commission.europa.eu/system/files/2018-02/emt_competence_fwk_2017_en_web.pdf.

European Union. 2019. 'EU Host Paper: New Technologies and Artificial Intelligence in the Field of Language and Conference Services'. https://commission.europa.eu/system/files/2019-06/final_host_paper_iamladp2019_en_version.pdf.

Garista, Patrizia, and Giancarlo Pocetta. 2014. *Digital Resilience: Meanings, Epistemologies and Methodologies for Lifelong Learning.* https://doi.org/10.13140/2.1.3552.1605.

Göpferich, Suzanne. 2009. 'Towards a Model of Translation Competence and Its Acquisition: The Longitudinal Study Transcomp'. In *Behind the Mind. Methods, Models and Results in Translation Process Research*, edited by Suzanne Göpferich, Arnt-Lykke Jakobsen, and Inger M. Mees, 11–37. Copenhagen: Samfundslitteratur Press.

Gouadec, Daniel. 2007. *Translation as a Profession.* Amsterdam/Philadelphia: John Benjamins. www.jbe-platform.com/content/books/9789027292513.

Guerberof Arenas, Ana. 2013. 'What Do Professional Translators Think about Post-Editing?' *Journal of Specialised Translation*, no. 19: 75–95.

———. 2019. 'Pre-Editing and Post-Editing'. In *The Bloomsbury Companion to Language Industry Studies*, edited by Erik Angelone, Maureen Ehrensberger-Dow, and Gary Massey, 333–60. Bloomsbury Publishing.

Guerberof Arenas, Ana, and Antonio Toral. 2020. 'The Impact of Post-Editing and Machine Translation on Creativity and Reading Experience'. *Translation Spaces* 9 (November). https://doi.org/10.1075/ts.20035.gue.

Guerberof-Arenas, Ana, and Joss Moorkens. 2023. 'Ethics and Machine Translation: The End User Perspective'. In *Towards Responsible Machine Translation: Ethical and Legal Considerations in Machine Translation*, edited by Helena Moniz and Carla Parra Escartín, 113–33. Springer Verlag.

Guerreiro, Nuno M., Duarte M. Alves, Jonas Waldendorf, Barry Haddow, Alexandra Birch, Pierre Colombo, and André F. T. Martins. 2023. 'Hallucinations in Large Multilingual Translation Models'. *Transactions of the Association for Computational Linguistics* 11 (December): 1500–1517. https://doi.org/10.1162/tacl_a_00615.

Hansen, Gyde. 2006. 'Retrospection Methods in Translator Training and Translation Research'. *Journal of Specialised Translation* 5 (1): 2–41.

Haro-Soler, María. (2017). 'Teaching Practices and Translation Students' Self-Efficacy: The Teachers' Perceptions.' *Current Trends in Translation Teaching and Learning* 4: 198–228.

———. 2018. 'Self-Confidence and Its Role in Translator Training: The Students' Perspective'. In *Innovation and Expansion in Translation Process Research*, edited by Isabel Lacruz and Riitta Jääskeläinen, 131–60. Amsterdam/Philadelphia: John Benjamins. https://doi.org/10.1075/ata. xviii.

———. 2019. 'Vicarious Learning in the Translation Classroom: How Can It Influence Students' Self-Efficacy Beliefs?' *English Studies at NBU* 5 (1): 92–113. https://doi.org/10.33919/esnbu.19.1.5.

———. (2021). 'Teachers' Feedback and Trainees' Confidence: Do They Match? *Research in Language* 19 (2): 187–210.

Haro-Soler, Maria del Mar, and Don Kiraly. 2019. 'Exploring Self-Efficacy Beliefs in Symbiotic Collaboration with Students: An Action Research Project'. *The Interpreter and Translator Trainer* 13 (3): 255–70. https://doi.org/10.1080/1750399X.2019.1656405.

Herbert, Sarah, Félix do Carmo, Joanna Gough, and Anu Carnegie-Brown. 2023. 'From Responsibilities to Responsibility: A Study of the Effects of Translation Workflow Automation'. *Journal of Specialised Translation* 40: 9–35.

Hobfoll, Stevan E. 2002. 'Social and Psychological Resources and Adaptation'. *Review of General Psychology* 6 (4): 307–24. https://doi.org/10.1037/1089-2680.6.4.307

Hobfoll, Stevan E., Robert J. Johnson, Nicole Ennis, and Anita P. Jackson. 2003. 'Resource Loss, Resource Gain, and Emotional Outcomes Among Inner City Women'. *Journal of Personality and Social Psychology* 84 (3): 632–43. https://doi.org/10.1037/0022-3514.84.3.632.

Hobfoll, Stevan, Jonathon Halbesleben, Jean-Pierre Neveu, and Mina Westman. 2018. 'Conservation of Resources in the Organizational Context: The Reality of Resources and Their Consequences'. *Annual Review of Organizational Psychology and Organizational Behavior* 5 (1): 103–28. https://doi.org/10.1146/annurev-orgpsych-032117-104640.

Holdsworth, Sarah, Michelle Turner, and Christina M. Scott-Young. 2018. '... Not Drowning, Waving. Resilience and University: A Student Perspective'. *Studies in Higher Education* 43 (11): 1837–53. https://doi.org/10.1080/03075079.2017.1284193.

Hubscher-Davidson, Séverine. 2009. 'Personal Diversity and Diverse Personalities in Translation: A Study of Individual Differences'. *Perspectives* 17 (3): 175–92. https://doi.org/10.1080/09076760903249380.

———. 2013. 'The Role of Intuition in the Translation Process: A Case Study'. *Translation and Interpreting Studies. The Journal of the American Translation and Interpreting Studies Association*. John Benjamins. https://doi.org/10.1075/tis.8.2.05hub.

———. 2017. *Translation and Emotion: A Psychological Perspective*. New York: Routledge. https://doi.org/10.4324/9781315720388.

———. 2020. 'Ethical Stress in the Translation and Interpreting Professions'. In *The Routledge Handbook of Translation and Ethics*, edited by Kaisa Koskinen and Nike K. Pokorn, 415–30. Routledge Handbooks. Abingdon: Routledge. www.routledge.com/The-Routledge-Handbook-of-Translation-and-Ethics/Koskinen-Pokorn/p/book/9780815358237.

Jääskeläinen, Riitta. 2012. 'Translation Psychology'. In *Handbook of Translation Studies: Volume 3*, edited by Yves Gambier and Luc van Doorslaer, 191–97. Handbook of Translation Studies. John Benjamins Publishing Company. https://doi.org/10.1075/hts.3.tra14.

James, William. 1890. *The Principles of Psychology, Vol I*. The Principles of Psychology, Vol I. New York, NY, US: Henry Holt and Co. https://doi.org/10.1037/10538-000.

Ji, Ziwei, Nayeon Lee, Rita Frieske, Tiezheng Yu, Dan Su, Yan Xu, Etsuko Ishii, Ye Jin Bang, Andrea Madotto, and Pascale Fung. 2023. 'Survey of Hallucination in Natural Language Generation'. *ACM Computing Surveys* 55 (12): 248:1–248:38. https://doi.org/10.1145/3571730.

Kelly, Dorothy. 2005. *A Handbook for Translator Trainers*. Routledge. www.routledge.com/A-Handbook-for-Translator-Trainers/Kelly/p/book/9781900650816.

———. 2007. 'Translator Competence Contextualized. Translator Training in the Framework of Higher Education Reform: In Search of Alignment in Curricular Design'. In *Across Boundaries: International Perspectives on Translation Studies*, edited by Dorothy Kenny and Ryou Kyongjoo. Newcastle: Cambridge Scholars Publishing. www.cambridgescholars.com/product/9781847182425.

Kinnunen, Tuija, and Kaisa Koskinen, eds. 2010. *Translators' Agency*. Vol. 4. Tampere: Tampere University Press.

Kiraly, Don. 1990. 'Toward a Systematic Approach to Translation Skills Instruction'. Text, University of Illinois at Urbana-Champaign. https://hdl.handle.net/2142/22213.

———. 2000. *A Social Constructivist Approach to Translator Education: Empowerment from Theory to Practice*. Manchester, UK.
Klimkowski, Konrad. 2015. *Towards a Shared Curriculum in Translator and Interpreter Education*. Wrocław: Wydawnictwo Wyższej Szkoły Filologicznej.
———. 2019. 'Assessment as a Communicative Activity in the Translation Classroom'. *Intralinea* Special Issue.
Köbis, Nils, and Luca D. Mossink. 2021. 'Artificial Intelligence versus Maya Angelou: Experimental Evidence That People Cannot Differentiate AI-Generated from Human-Written Poetry'. *Computers in Human Behavior* 114 (January): 106553. https://doi.org/10.1016/j.chb.2020.106553.
Koponen, Maarit. 2016. 'Is Machine Translation Post-Editing Worth the Effort? A Survey of Research into Post-Editing and Effort'. *The Journal of Specialised Translation* 25 (2): 131–48.
Krings, Hans P. 2001. 'Repairing Texts: Empirical Investigations of Machine Translation Post-Editing Processes'. https://api.semanticscholar.org/CorpusID:60041700.
Krüger, Ralph. 2022. 'Integrating Professional Machine Translation Literacy and Data Literacy'. *Lebende Sprachen* 67 (2): 247–82. https://doi.org/10.1515/les-2022-1022.
Kußmaul, Paul. 1995. *Training the Translator*. Amsterdam: John Benjamins. https://doi.org/10.1075/btl.10.
LeBlanc, Matthieu. 2017. '"I Can't Get No Satisfaction!" Should We Blame Translation Technologies or Shifting Business Practices?' In *Human Issues in Translation Technology*, edited by Dorothy Kenny, 45–62. London: Routledge.
Lee, Tong King. 2023. 'Artificial Intelligence and Posthumanist Translation: Chatgpt Versus the Translator', Applied Linguistics Review, https://doi.org/10.1515/applirev-2023-0122.
Lengnick-Hall, Cynthia A., and Tammy E. Beck. 2005. 'Adaptive Fit Versus Robust Transformation: How Organizations Respond to Environmental Change'. *Journal of Management* 31 (5): 738–57. https://doi.org/10.1177/0149206305279367.
Lester, Brian, Rami Al-Rfou, and Noah Constant. 2021. 'The Power of Scale for Parameter-Efficient Prompt Tuning'. arXiv. https://doi.org/10.48550/arXiv.2104.08691
Massey, Gary, and Maureen Ehrensberger-Dow. 2017. 'Machine Learning: Implications for Translator Education', Lebende Sprachen, 62 (2): 300–312. https://doi.org/10.1515/les-2017-0021.
Masten, A. S., and J. D. Coatsworth. 1998. 'The Development of Competence in Favorable and Unfavorable Environments. Lessons from Research on Successful Children'. *The American Psychologist* 53 (2): 205–20. https://doi.org/10.1037//0003-066x.53.2.205.

Miyata, Rei, and Atsushi Fujita. 2021. 'Understanding Pre-Editing for Black-Box Neural Machine Translation', February. https://arxiv.org/abs/2102.02955v1.

Muñoz Martín, Ricardo. 2010. 'Leave No Stone Unturned. on the Development of Cognitive Translatology'. *Translation and Interpreting Studies* 5 (August): 145–62. https://doi.org/10.1075/tis.5.2.01mun.

———. 2013. 'Cognitive and Psycholinguistic Approaches'. In *The Routledge Handbook of Translation Studies*, edited by Carmen Millán and Francesca Bartrina, 241–56. New York: Routledge.

———. 2014. 'Situating Translation Expertise: A Review with a Sketch of a Construct'. In *The Development of Translation Competence: Theories and Methodologies from Psycholinguistics and Cognitive Science*, edited by John W. Schwieter and Aline Ferreira, 2–56. Newcastle: Cambridge Scholars Publishing.

Muñoz-Basols, Javier, Craig Neville, Barbara A. Lafford, and Concepción Godev. 2023. 'Potentialities of Applied Translation for Language Learning in the Era of Artificial Intelligence'. *Hispania* 106 (2): 171–94.

Muñoz Martín, Ricardo, and César Andrés González Fernández. 2021. 'Cognitive Translatology: A Primer, Revisited'. *Studies in Language, Communication and Cognition* 1 (1): 131–65.

Muñoz Martín, Ricardo, and Christian Olalla-Soler. 2022. 'Translating Is Not (Only) Problem Solving'. *The Journal of Specialised Translation* 38 (July): 1–26.

Newmark, Peter. 1988. *A Textbook of Translation*. New York and London: Prentice Hall.

Nida, Eugene A. 1964. *Toward a Science of Translating*. Leiden: E. J. Brill.

Nitzke, Jean, and Silvia Hansen-Schirra. 2021. *A Short Guide to Post-Editing*. Language Science Press. Language Science Press. https://doi.org/10.5281/zenodo.5646896.

Nof, Shimon. 2009. 'Automation: What It Means to Us Around the World'. In *Springer Handbook of Automation*, 13–52. https://doi.org/10.1007/978-3-540-78831-7_3.

Norberg, Ulf. 2014. 'Fostering Self-Reflection in Translation Students: The Value of Guided Commentaries'. *Translation and Interpreting Studies* 9 (1): 150–64.

Núñez, Juan L., and Alicia Bolaños-Medina. 2018. 'Predictors of Problem-Solving in Translation: Implications for Translator Training'. *The Interpreter and Translator Trainer* 12 (3): 282–98. https://doi.org/10.1080/1750399X.2017.1359762.

O'Brien, Sharon. 2002. 'Teaching Post-Editing: A Proposal for Course Content'. In *Proceedings of the 6th EAMT Workshop: Teaching Machine Translation*. Manchester, England: European Association for Machine Translation. https://aclanthology.org/2002.eamt-1.11.

O'Brien, Sharon, Maureen Ehrensberger-Dow, Megan Connolly, and Marcel Hasler. 2017. 'Irritating CAT Tool Features That Matter to Translators'. *HERMES – Journal of Language and Communication in Business*, no. 56 (October): 145–62. https://doi.org/10.7146/hjlcb.v0i56.97229.

O'Brien, Sharon, and Alessandra Rossetti. 2020. 'Neural Machine Translation and the Evolution of the Localisation Sector: Implications for Training'. *The Journal of Internationalization and Localization*. John Benjamins. https://doi.org/10.1075/jial.20005.obr.

Olohan, Maeve. 2016. *Scientific and Technical Translation*. London: Routledge. https://doi.org/10.4324/9781315679600.

PACTE. 2003. 'Building a Translation Competence Model'. In *Triangulating Translation: Perspectives in Process Oriented Research*, edited by Fabio Alves, 43–66. Amsterdam/Philadelphia: John Benjamins Publishing Company.

———. 2008. 'First Results of a Translation Competence Experiment: Knowledge of Translation and Efficacy of the Translation Process'. In *Translator and Interpreter Training. Issues, Methods and Debates*, edited by John Kearns, 104–26. London: Continuum.

Peng, Keqin, Liang Ding, Qihuang Zhong, Li Shen, Xuebo Liu, Min Zhang, Yuanxin Ouyang, and Dacheng Tao. 2023. 'Towards Making the Most of ChatGPT for Machine Translation'. SSRN Scholarly Paper. Rochester, NY. https://doi.org/10.2139/ssrn.4390455.

Pietrzak, Paulina. 2018. 'The Effects of Students' Self-Regulation on Translation Quality'. *Babel. Revue Internationale de La Traduction / International Journal of Translation* 64 (5–6): 819–39. https://doi.org/10.1075/babel.00064.pie.

———. 2022. *Metacognitive Translator Training. Focus on Personal Resources*. London: Palgrave.

Pietrzak, Paulina, and Michał Kornacki. 2021. *Using CAT Tools in Freelance Translation: Insights from a Case Study*. Routledge. https://doi.org/10.4324/9781003125761.

Pokrivcakova, Silvia. 2019. 'Preparing Teachers for the Application of AI-Powered Technologies in Foreign Language Education'. *Journal of Language and Cultural Education* 7 (3): 135–53.

Pym, Anthony. 2004. *The Moving Text: Localization, Translation, and Distribution. Anthony Pym*. John Benjamins. https://doi.org/10.1075/btl.49

Pym, Anthony, and Ester Torres-Simón. 2021. 'Is Automation Changing the Translation Profession?' *International Journal of the Sociology of Language* 2021 (270): 39–57. https://doi.org/10.1515/ijsl-2020-0015.

Reynolds, Laria, and Kyle McDonell. 2021. 'Prompt Programming for Large Language Models: Beyond the Few-Shot Paradigm'. arXiv. https://doi.org/10.48550/arXiv.2102.07350.

Risku, Hanna, and Daniela Schlager. 2022. 'Epistemologies of Translation Expertise: Notions in Research and Praxis'. In *Contesting Epistemologies in Cognitive Translation and Interpreting Studies*, edited by Sandra L. Halverson and Álvaro Marín García, 11–31. New York: Routledge.

Saldanha, Gabriela, and Sharon O'Brien. 2013. 'Research Methodologies in Translation Studies'. Routledge & CRC Press. 2013. www.routledge.com/Research-Methodologies-in-Translation-Studies/Saldanha-OBrien/p/book/9781909485006.

Sánchez-Gijón, Pilar, and Dorothy Kenny. 2022. 'Selecting and Preparing Texts for Machine Translation: Pre-Editing and Writing for a Global Audience'. In *Machine Translation for Everyone: Empowering Users in the Age of Artificial Intelligence*, edited by Dorothy Kenny, 81–103. Berlin: Language Science Press. https://doi.org/10.5281/zenodo.6759980.

Schäffner, Christina. 2020. 'Translator's Roles and Responsibilities'. In *The Bloomsbury Companion to Language Industry Studies*, edited by Erik Angelone, Maureen Ehrensberger-Dow, and Gary Massey, 63–89. London: Bloomsbury.

Shavelson, Richard J., Judith J. Hubner, and George C. Stanton. 1976. 'Self-Concept: Validation of Construct Interpretations'. *Review of Educational Research* 46 (3): 407–41. https://doi.org/10.2307/1170010.

Shreve, Gregory. 2006. 'The Deliberate Practice: Translation and Expertise'. *Journal of Translation Studies* 9 (1): 27–42.

———. 2009. 'Recipient-Orientation and Metacognition in the Translation Process'. In *Translators and Their Readers. In Homage to Eugene A. Nida*, edited by Rodica Dimitriu and Miriam Shlesinger, 255–70. Brussels: Editions du Hazard.

Skinner, Ellen A. 1996. 'A Guide to the Construct of Control'. *Journal of Personality and Social Psychology* 71: 549–70.

Škobo, Milena, and Vedran Petričević. 2023. 'Navigating the Challenges and Opportunities of Literary Translation in the Age of AI: Striking a Balance Between Human Expertise and Machine Power'. *DHS* 2: 317–36.

Svahn, Elin. 2016. 'Feeling Like a Translator: Exploring Translator Students' Self-Concepts Through Focus Groups'. In *New Horizons in Translation Research and Education 4*, edited by Turo Rautaoja, Tamara Mikolič Južnič, and Kaisa Koskinen, 27–45. Joensuu: University of Eastern Finland.

Thoits, Peggy. 1994. 'Stressors and Problem-Solving: The Individual as Psychological Activist'. *Journal of Health and Social Behavior* 35: 143–60.

Tiselius, Elisabeth, and Adelina Hild. 2017. 'Expertise and Competence in Translation and Interpreting'. In *The Handbook of Translation and Cognition*, edited by John W. Schwieter and Aline Ferreira, 425–44. West Sussex: Wiley-Blackwell.

Tomarenko, Valerij. 2019. *Through the Client's Eyes: How to Make Your Translations Visible.* Berlin BDÜ Fachverlag.

Torrejón, Enrique, and Celia Rico. 2013. 'Skills and Profile of the New Role of the Translator as MT Post-Editor'. *Tradumàtica: Tecnologies de La Traducció*, February, 166. https://doi.org/10.5565/rev/tradumatica.18.

Vieira, Lucas Nunes. 2020. 'Automation Anxiety and Translators'. *Translation Studies* 13 (1): 1–21. https://doi.org/10.1080/14781700.2018.1543613.

Walczyński, Marcin. 2021. '"Will I Make It or Will I Make a Fool of Myself": Polish-English Certified Interpreters' Experience of Anxiety'. *Onomázein*, no. NEVIII (May): 83–103. https://doi.org/10.7764/onomazein.ne8.03.

Walker, Caroline, Alan Gleaves, and John Grey. 2006. 'Can Students Within Higher Education Learn to Be Resilient and, Educationally Speaking, Does It Matter?' *Educational Studies* 32 (3): 251–64. https://doi.org/10.1080/03055690600631184.

Wiener, Earl L. 1989. 'Human Factors of Advanced Technology (Glass Cockpit) Transport Aircraft'. NAS 1.26:177528. https://ntrs.nasa.gov/citations/19890016609.

Wu, Tongshuang, Michael Terry, and Carrie Jun Cai. 2022. 'AI Chains: Transparent and Controllable Human-AI Interaction by Chaining Large Language Model Prompts'. In *Proceedings of the 2022 CHI Conference on Human Factors in Computing Systems*, 1–22. New York,: Association for Computing Machinery. https://doi.org/10.1145/3491102.3517582.

4 Attitudes towards AI in translation
An academic exploration

4.1 Research design

The methodology of the study is structured around a quantitative analysis of the perceptions and attitudes of translation professionals, academics and students towards the integration of GenAI in translation and translator education. To achieve a comprehensive understanding, the research utilised the Computer-Assisted Web Interview (CAWI) approach, targeting a diverse group that includes practicing translators, translator educators and translation trainees. Conducted between late 2023 and early 2024, this strategy facilitated the distribution of a detailed survey designed to gather data on respondents' views regarding the use of AI technology in translation processes, the necessity of incorporating GenAI into translator education and the potential effects of such technologies on translator training. This approach enabled the collection of rich data, ensuring a broad spectrum of perspectives was considered.

Upon collecting the survey data, the study employed the Statistical Package for the Social Sciences (SPSS) for data analysis, adopting quantitative correlational methods to assess the attitudes towards AI in translation and translator education. The aims of the study focus on exploring the spectrum of perspectives within the translation community concerning GenAI, aiming to understand its perceived role, challenges and opportunities. Since the study aims to explore expert and student approaches to the growing use of AI technologies in translation, guiding future education and professional development, the objectives include:

1 Evaluating the current perceptions and attitudes towards GenAI use in both translation practices and translator education among professionals, academics and students.
2 Identifying significant patterns or trends in GenAI attitudes across different groups within the translation community (i.e., professionals, educators and students).
3 Evaluating the perceived necessity and potential impact of integrating GenAI into translator training, with a focus on implications for the profession and education.

The statistical analysis allowed for identifying patterns and trends in how different stakeholder groups perceive the role and implications of GenAI in the field (see Section 4.3).

The analysis was conducted using basic descriptive statistics such as mean, median, standard deviation and skewness. Preferences regarding translation tools were presented using relationship maps. Statistical tests were also employed to compare two or more populations. These included the Kruskal-Wallis test (with post hoc tests), the chi-square test of independence, the Z test for proportion and the t-test for correlation. The effect size was evaluated using the Spearman rho coefficient or the Cramer's V coefficient. When analysing threats related to GenAI, the reliability of the measurement method was assessed using Cronbach's alpha coefficient. Furthermore, exploratory factor analysis was utilised. The extraction of common variability was carried out using the principal component method, that is, an adaptation of the method developed by Hotelling for the purposes of factor analysis (Walesiak & Gatnar, 2009). The number of factors was determined based on Kaiser's criterion (eigenvalue greater than 1) (Wiktorowicz 2016: 299). All data were reviewed and analysed with the help of an expert statistician.[1]

4.2 Limitations of the study

The study presents several limitations that are important to consider for a comprehensive understanding of the findings. First, the use of the CAWI approach, while advantageous for reaching a diverse group of participants across different locations, may introduce selection bias. This bias occurs as the method inherently favours individuals with the willingness to participate in online surveys, potentially excluding perspectives from those without such inclination. Consequently, the results might not fully represent the broader community of translation professionals, academics and students, particularly those from those less inclined towards online engagement.

Additionally, the demographic characteristics of the sample, despite efforts to encompass a wide range of participants, may not fully capture the diversity within the translation community. Factors such as age, geographical location, level of professional experience and field of specialisation can significantly influence perceptions of technology. If certain groups are underrepresented in the survey data, the study's conclusions might not adequately reflect the nuanced views across the entire spectrum of the translation profession and academia. Thus, the demographic diversity of the sample may not fully represent the entire translation community. Nonetheless, the study still captures a wide range of perspectives from professionals, academics and students involved in translation. This diversity is crucial for understanding the multifaceted views on GenAI and provides a foundation for future research. The insights gained can potentially contribute to both academic discussions and practical applications, guiding the development of curricula and tools that better align with the needs and expectations of translation stakeholders.

Another potential limitation of the study is the temporal scope of the data collection, conducted between November 2023 and January 2024, which might influence the attitudes and perceptions captured by the study. During this period, specific events or developments in the field of GenAI and translation technology might have temporarily swayed opinions, leading to responses that reflect situational factors rather than stable, long-term attitudes. Given the dynamic changes in AI technologies, the findings may offer a snapshot of perceptions within a specific timeframe, which might evolve as the integration of GenAI in translation practices and education continues to develop.

This leads to another limitation. While the focus is mainly on the practical implications and perceptions of GenAI, it does not fully address the ethical concerns or biases that are raised by the use of AI technologies. The data used to train AI can often reflect historical biases or disparities, which can be perpetuated and magnified by the AI systems if not addressed (e.g. gender bias in language use or cultural insensitivity). These issues are ethical in nature and may have a profound impact on the quality of GenAI-assisted translation if left unchecked. While the authors left space for respondents to freely share their thoughts in the final optional open-ended question of the survey, they acknowledge that integrating qualitative research methods, such as detailed interviews, would allow for a better understanding of how people perceive these technologies and the ethical challenges they pose, including the potential job takeover by AI.

Despite the above-mentioned limitations of data collection potentially capturing only immediate reactions to developments in GenAI with no deeper exploration, the authors believe the findings are invaluable and may serve as a benchmark for future research as they offer insights into the translation community's initial responses to technological advancements. This snapshot facilitates understanding of how professionals, academics and students adapt to and perceive GenAI, informing the development of responsive technologies, curricula and policies. Moreover, it highlights the community's adaptability and potential areas of resistance, guiding targeted strategies for inclusive and beneficial integration of GenAI into translation practices and education, thus laying a foundation for ongoing discourse and development in the rapidly evolving field of GenAI and translation.

Finally, the statistical analysis, while comprehensive in employing basic descriptive statistics (mean, median, standard deviation, skewness), relationship maps, and a variety of statistical tests (Kruskal-Wallis with post hoc tests, chi-square test of independence, Z test for proportion, t-test for correlation), still encounters several methodological challenges. It must be acknowledged that the reliance on descriptive statistics and relationship maps to present user preferences regarding translation tools might not capture the full complexity of users' attitudes and behaviours. While these methods are effective in illustrating general trends and preferences, they may overlook nuanced understanding or the underlying reasons behind these preferences. The authors acknowledge not only the importance of exploring alternative or complementary statistical approaches in future research, but also – more importantly perhaps – the need for critical engagement with the results, acknowledging the constraints under which these statistical findings are interpreted and applied within the context of attitudes towards GenAI in translation and translator education.

4.3 Data analysis

The data analysis section presents findings collected from the survey conducted within the translation community. Regarding the

Table 4.1 Demographic structure of the sample (n = 151)

Characteristics		Sample	
		n	%
Role/profession	Translator	54	35.8
	Translation teacher	43	28.5
	Translation student	54	35.8
Age	20–29	53	35.1
	30–39	23	15.2
	40–49	37	24.5
	50+	38	25.2

demographic characteristics of the sample, the survey targeted expert translators and translator educators, including both individuals and those associated with the Consortium for Translation Education Research (CTER), as well as members of relevant forums (ProZ) and professional groups on Groups.io. Additionally, it reached out to students from the University of Łódź, Poland, who specialise in translation.

Out of those contacted, 151 participants completed the questionnaire, providing a dataset for analysis.

The participants spanned a range of roles within the translation field, including translation professionals, educators and students, reflecting a wide spectrum of experiences and perspectives on the integration of GenAI in translation processes and education. This variation in participant backgrounds is crucial for the study, as it aims to explore and compare the attitudes and perceptions of different stakeholders within the translation community.

The following sections of the data analysis present the findings on the use of AI technologies in translation (Section 4.3.1) and survey opinions on GenAI integration in translator education (Section 4.3.2).

4.3.1 Findings on the use of AI technologies in translation

As for the use of AI technology, the majority of respondents reported using Machine Translation (MT) (77.3%) and Translation Management Systems (TMS[2]) (60.0%) as their primary AI-powered tools. Nearly half of the participants indicated the use of writing assistants and checking tools (46.7%). The use of these tools significantly varies by role/profession, though the association is weak (Cramer's V coefficient ranging from 0.5 to 0.3) (see Table 4.2).

Tools from the first group (MT) were significantly more often indicated by translation students (91%) than translators (67%, p = 0.007), whereas the differences between other groups are not statistically significant. Conversely, TMS tools are significantly less frequently used by translation teachers (38%) compared to translators and translation students (67–70%), while writing assistants and checking tools are significantly less frequently used by translators (28%) compared to translation teachers and students (56–59%). GenAI tools were indicated much less frequently – 28.7% of respondents mentioned AI, with no significant difference in role/profession (in the chi-square test, p = 0.264 > α, V = 0.133 – see Table 4.2), nor age (p = 0.110, V = 0.200 – see Table 4.3). Only a small number of respondents reported not using any of the discussed tools (6% overall), with translation teachers being the most frequent non-users (14%).

The use of the discussed solutions is affected by age, except for GenAI, which remains unaffected. Significant differences are observed regarding the use of machine translation tools among different age groups. Specifically, younger individuals aged 20–29 and 30–39 years tend to use these tools more frequently than those aged 40–49 and 50 years and over. However, there are no noteworthy differences between people in their twenties and thirties, as well as between those in their forties and older. There are some differences in the use of TMS among different age groups, which are weak but statistically significant (p = 0.015, V = 0.263). People aged 30–39 use it less frequently (35%) than the youngest and oldest age groups (about 70% each). The youngest age group (20–29) uses writing assistants and checking tools nearly twice as often as the oldest age group (59% vs. 30%). While individuals aged 40–49 indicated the use of GenAI more frequently than other age groups (43% compared to 21–30%), the differences are not statistically significant. Almost all individuals aged 20–29 and 95% of those aged 30–39 use at least one of these solutions, while about one in ten individuals aged 40 and over did not mention any of the discussed tools (see Table 4.3).

A further 13.2% of the respondents indicated the use of tools from all four groups, 21.2% from three of them, the majority – 35.8% – from two of them, and 23.2% from just one (Table 4.4). When opting for a single solution, it was usually MT (half of those using one solution) or TMS (a third of them), less frequently GenAI (one in ten), and even

Table 4.2 AI-powered tools used in translation (total and by role/profession)

	Total		Role/profession						Chi-square test			V	Pair differences (Z test)
			Translator (T)		Translation teacher (TT)		Translation student (TS)						
	n	%	n	%	n	%	n	%	χ^2	df	p		
Translation Management Systems (TMS), e.g. Trados, Phrase, MemoQ etc.	90	60.0	38	70.4	16	38.1	36	66.7	12.675	2	0.002**	0.290	T > TT (p = 0.005**) TS > TT (p = 0.016**)
Machine translation, e.g. DeepL, Microsoft Translator, Google Translate, Amazon Cloud etc.	116	77.3	36	66.7	31	73.8	49	90.7	9.543	2	0.008**	0.251	TS > T (p = 0.007**)
Generative AI, e.g. ChatGPT, Google Bard, etc.	43	28.7	15	27.8	16	38.1	12	22.2	2.660	2	0.264	0.133	n.a.
Writing assistants and checking tools, e.g. Grammarly, Microsoft Editor etc.	70	46.7	15	27.8	25	59.5	30	55.6	11.734	2	0.003**	0.279	TT > T (p = 0.005**) TS > T (p=0.010*)
None of the above	9	6.0	3	5.6	6	14.3	0	0.0	8.340	2	0.008**	0.235	TT > TS (p = 0.006**)

* $p < 0.05$, ** $p < 0.01$, *** $p < 0.001$. V – V-Cramer coefficient, p – probability in chi-square/Z test, df – degree of freedom.

Table 4.3 AI-powered tools used in translation (total and by age)

	Age								Chi-square test			V	Pair differences (Z test)
	20–29 (A)		30–39 (B)		40–49 (C)		50+ (D)						
	n	%	n	%	n	%	n	%	χ^2	df	p		
Translation Management Systems, e.g. Trados, Phrase, MemoQ etc.	37	69.8	8	34.8	19	51.4	26	70.3	10.452	3	0.015*	0.263	A > B (p = 0.026*) D > B (p = 0.042*)
Machine translation, e.g. DeepL, Microsoft Translator, Google Translate, Amazon Cloud etc.	49	92.5	22	95.7	23	62.2	22	59.5	23.963	3	<0.001***	0.398	A > C (p = 0.002**) A > D (p = 0.001**) B > C (p = 0.021*) B > D (p = 0.012*)
Generative AI, e.g. ChatGPT, Google Bard, etc.	11	20.8	5	21.7	16	43.2	11	29.7	6.030	3	0.110	0.200	n.a.
Writing assistants and checking tools, e.g. Grammarly, Microsoft Editor etc.	31	58.5	11	47.8	17	45.9	11	29.7	7.792	3	0.048*	0.227	A > D (p = 0.043*)
None of the above	0	0.0	1	4.3	4	10.8	4	10.8	6.432	3	0.085	0.206	n.a.

* p < 0.05, ** p < 0.01, *** p < 0.001. V – V-Cramer coefficient, p – probability in chi-square/Z test, df – degree of freedom.

86 Attitudes towards AI in translation

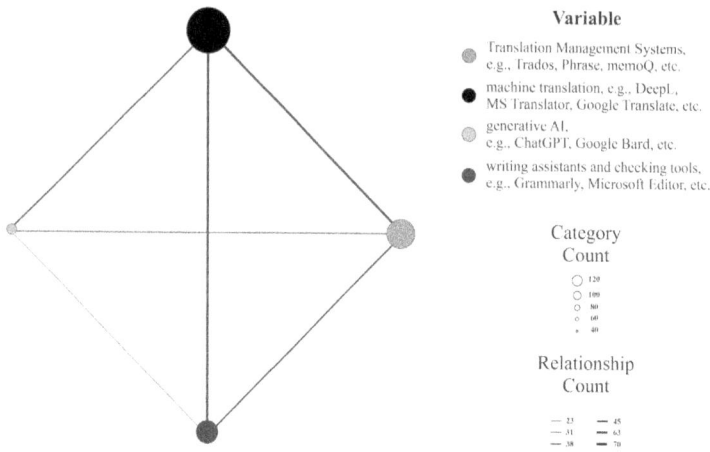

Figure 4.1 Relationship map.

less so – writing assistants and checking tools (one in 20). All those using three solutions included machine translation. Among them, 90% also included TMS, 72% included writing assistants and checking tools and 38% included GenAI. When opting for two solutions, these were primarily machine translation (87% of these individuals) and TMS (52%) or writing assistants and checking tools (46%), less frequently GenAI (15%). These connections are illustrated in Figure 4.1.

Out of all translation teachers surveyed, every fifth one reported using all four solution groups, which is twice as often as the other two groups. Most translators tend to rely on one or two solutions (35% and 32%, respectively), while students use two (49%) or three (32%). Translation teachers' opinions vary more widely (16–26% indicating individual tools). The most significant differences are observed between translators and translation students ($p = 0.082$ in the post hoc test). However, at the significance level of $\alpha = 0.05$, there is no statistically significant difference between the use of these tools based on the role/profession ($p = 0.080$) – as shown in Table 4.4.

Age is a clear differentiating factor ($p = 0.053$) in the holistic use of these tools, with the youngest (20–29 years) and oldest (50+ years, $p = 0.069$) showing the greatest differences. Individuals aged 20–29 tend to use a significantly more varied range of tools compared to those aged 50+ (see Table 4.4).

Table 4.4 Number of tools in use by role/profession and age

Number of tools		Role/profession (p = 0.080)			Age (p = 0.053)			
		Translator	Translation teacher	Translation student	20–29 (A)	30–39 (B)	40–49 (C)	50+ (D)
None or n.a.	n	3	7	0	0	1	4	5
	%	5.6	16.3	0.0	0.0	4.3	10.8	13.2
1	n	19	9	7	5	6	12	12
	%	35.2	20.9	13.0	9.4	26.1	32.4	31.6
2	n	17	11	26	26	11	8	9
	%	31.5	25.6	48.1	49.1	47.8	21.6	23.7
3	n	9	7	16	17	2	5	8
	%	16.7	16.3	29.6	32.1	8.7	13.5	21.1
4	n	6	9	5	5	3	8	4
	%	11.1	20.9	9.3	9.4	13.0	21.6	10.5

p – probability in Kruskal-Wallis test.

88 Attitudes towards AI in translation

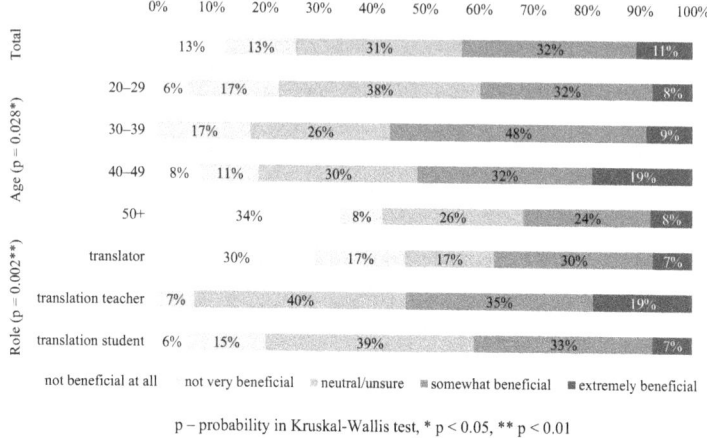

Figure 4.2 Perceived benefits of GenAI (e.g. ChatGPT) for translation (total and by age and role).
Note: p – probability in Kruskal-Wallis test, * $p < 0.05$, ** $p < 0.01$.

Almost half of the respondents believe that GenAI can bring benefits for translation. However, only one in ten people strongly confirm this, while about one in four thinks that it is not beneficial (see Figure 4.2). The average rating in this regard is 3.15 (with a standard deviation of 1.17), and the median is 3. The distribution's skewness is slight (S = -0.38). Both role/profession (p = 0.002) and age (p = 0.028) have a significant impact on people's opinions about GenAI.

Translation teachers expressed the most optimistic views on this topic, with 54% of them seeing benefits, including 19% decidedly, and only 7% not seeing them. The mean rating for this group is 3.65, with a standard deviation of 0.87 and a median of 4. Conversely, translators are the least optimistic, with almost half of them not seeing any benefits from GenAI. Their mean rating is 2.69, with a standard deviation of 1.37 and a median of 3. The differences between these two groups are statistically significant (p = 0.001 in the post hoc test).

In terms of age, respondents aged 30–49 expressed the most optimistic views, with a higher percentage of those who decidedly confirmed the benefits among individuals in their forties. Post hoc tests indicate that individuals aged 50 and above differ the most

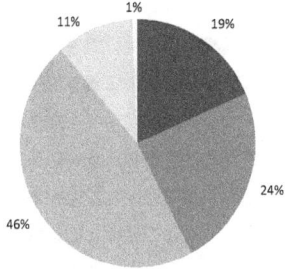

Figure 4.3 Perceived impact of GenAI on the translation market (shown in percentage).

(M = 2.63, SD = 1.38, Me = 3) compared to those in their forties (M = 3.43, SD = 1.17, Me = 4, p = 0.047) and thirties (M = 3.48, SD = 0.90, Me = 4, p = 0.088), but not twenties (M = 3.19, SD = 1.00, Me = 3, p = 0.464). The differences between the remaining groups are not statistically significant.

Respondents are rather sceptical regarding the impact of GenAI on the translation market – nearly half (43%) believe it will be negative, and only 12% that it will be positive. Nearly half of the respondents see both positive and negative effects in this regard (see Figure 4.3). The average is relatively low – on a scale of 1–5, it amounts to 2.51 (SD = 0.94), Me = 3. Again, translators are the most critical – nearly 60% of them see only the negative aspects of GenAI, and only 8% – positive ones.

The share of individuals indicating negative effects is smallest in the case of translation teachers (28%). Nevertheless, the share of those indicating benefits is similar for translators, especially students (13–14%). Role/profession significantly differentiates opinions in this regard (p = 0.003; see Figure 4.4). Post hoc tests indicate statistically significant differences between translators and translation teachers (p = 0.010) and students (p = 0.011), while translation teachers and students have similar opinions (M = 2.70, Me = 3, whereas for translators M = 2.17, Me = 2).

The impact of age on opinions is somewhat minimal (p = 0.060), but those aged 30–39 tend to have the most positive views (with 22% negative evaluations and 17% positive, showing the largest differences compared to those aged 50+ – p = 0.082). Interestingly,

90 *Attitudes towards AI in translation*

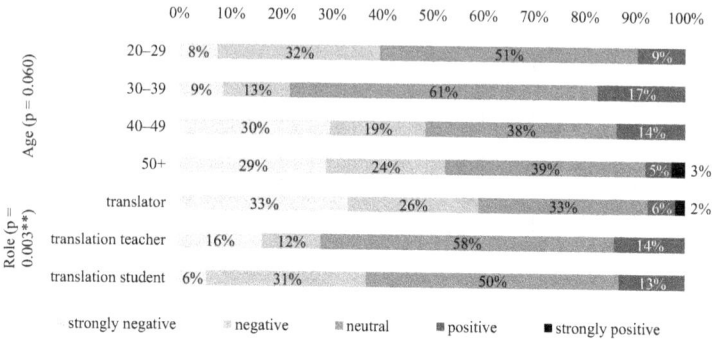

Figure 4.4 Impact of GenAI on the translation market: perspectives by role/profession and age (shown in percentage).

a large proportion of younger individuals (under 40) hold neutral opinions (51–61%). It is worth noting that opinions indicating a positive impact of AI on the market were most prevalent among those in their thirties and forties (14–17% compared to 8–9% for those in their twenties and over 50) – as shown in Figure 4.4. On average, those in their thirties had a relatively higher score (M = 2.87, Me = 3), while those aged 50+ had the lowest (M = 2.29, Me = 2).

Opinions on the impact of GenAI on translations and the translation market reveal a significant positive correlation (Spearman's rho = 0.365, p < 0.001). Individuals who view GenAI's impact on translations positively are likely to have a similar outlook on its influence on the translation market, while those sceptical of GenAI tend to be consistently critical across both areas. However, this correlation is "only" moderate in strength (see Figure 4.5).

Interestingly, there are some respondents who see a positive impact of GenAI on the translation market despite having a negative view on AI's impact on translation, although they are in the minority. Most of those who see no benefits from AI also have strong concerns about its negative impact on the translation market. Conversely, those who see significant benefits from AI tend to also see positive aspects for the translation market. Notably, responses indicating a negative impact on the translation market decrease as the assessment of AI's impact on translations (quality, etc.) becomes more positive, although neutral responses are still common.

Attitudes towards AI in translation 91

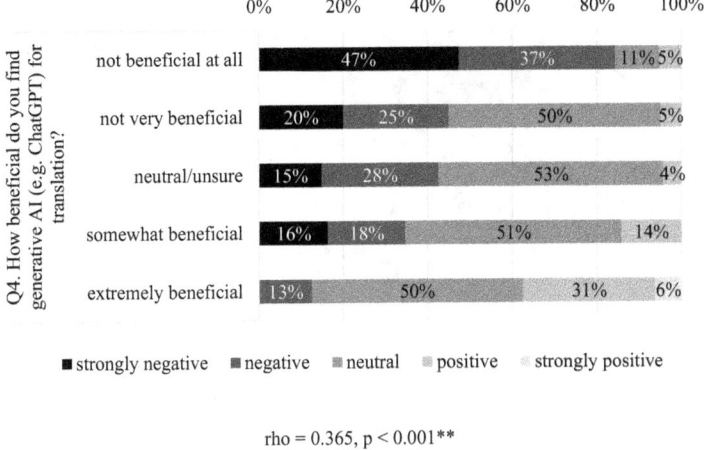

Figure 4.5 Impact of GenAI on translation and translation market (shown in percentage).

Note: rho = 0.365, p < 0.001**.

4.3.2 Perspectives on GenAI integration in translator education

Overall, perceptions regarding the integration of GenAI in translator education are generally favourable, with over half of positive responses affirming support for this matter (54%) and around a third (31%) expressing a neutral stance.

The average rating comes in at 3.52, with a standard deviation of 1.16 and a median of 4. Notably, opinions on this topic are not significantly linked to one's profession or role (p = 0.166), and age is also not a significant factor (p = 0.922; see Table 4.5).

Regarding the question on the extent to which GenAI tools, such as ChatGPT, should be used in translator training, a considerable proportion of respondents (46% with limited or small importance and 38% with moderate importance) demonstrate scepticism towards the value of incorporating GenAI tools into translator training.

The average rating was 3.52 (SD = 1.16, Me = 4). Interestingly, the results showed no significant association between this approach and role/profession (p = 0.073) or age (p = 0.951). However, it was found that translators and translation teachers had different opinions, with the former group showing lower evaluations (p = 0.066). Nevertheless,

92 Attitudes towards AI in translation

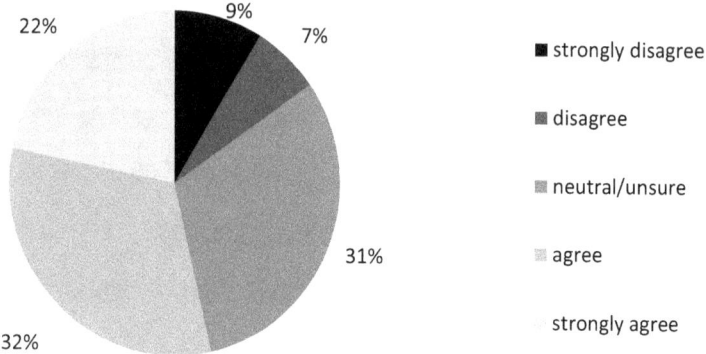

Figure 4.6 Perspectives on the integration of GenAI tools into translator training programmes (shown in percentage).

it is worth noting that a higher percentage of translators (9%) than others (2–5%) considered extensive use of AI to be a vital resource in training. Translation teachers had a relatively larger percentage of "moderate" answers (nearly 50%) and fewer "low" responses (28%).

Regarding the question of whether translation educators should be trained to use generative AI for teaching, the general consensus leans significantly towards agreement, with mostly positive (75%) or neutral (21%) attitudes. Only a small minority of respondents (less than 10%) believe that translation educators should not receive training in this area (see Figure 4.8). On average, the rating is 3.88 (SD = 1.03), with a median of 4.

Significant differences exist in the attitudes of translation teachers, students and professional translators towards the use of GenAI in education (post hoc test, p = 0.006 and p = 0.004, respectively). Translation teachers express a stronger desire to incorporate GenAI into their teaching (Kruskal-Wallis test, p = 0.002; see Table 4.7), with an average rating ranging from 3.61 (translators) to 4.35 (translation teachers).

These results underscore the enthusiasm among translation educators for embracing GenAI tools, suggesting they recognise potential benefits such as enhanced teaching methodologies or improved student engagement. Conversely, the more cautious stance of translators and students indicates a possible need for further

Table 4.5 Levels of agreement on GenAI tools integration into translator training programmes (by role/profession and age)

		Role/profession (p = 0.166)			Age (p = 0.922)			
		Translator	Translation teacher	Translation student	20–29 (A)	30–39 (B)	40–49 (C)	50+ (D)
strongly disagree	n	9	1	3	2	1	3	7
	%	16.7	2.3	5.6	3.8	4.3	8.1	18.4
disagree	n	4	2	4	4	3	2	1
	%	7.4	4.7	7.4	7.5	13.0	5.4	2.6
neutral/unsure	n	15	15	17	18	8	12	9
	%	27.8	34.9	31.5	34.0	34.8	32.4	23.7
agree	n	15	11	22	22	6	9	11
	%	27.8	25.6	40.7	41.5	26.1	24.3	28.9
strongly agree	n	11	14	8	7	5	11	10
	%	20.4	32.6	14.8	13.2	21.7	29.7	26.3

p – probability in Kruskal-Wallis test.

94 Attitudes towards AI in translation

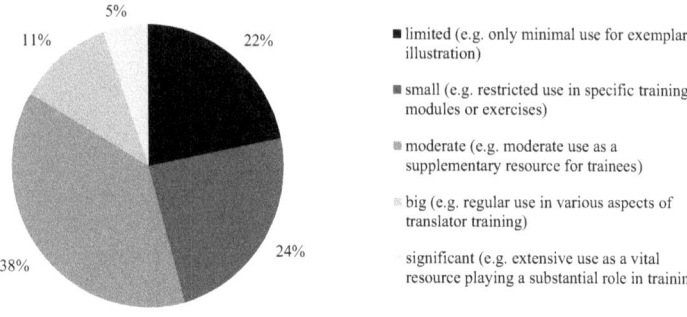

Figure 4.7 Responses on the extent to which GenAI tools (e.g. ChatGPT) should be used in translator training.

dialogue and education on GenAI's practical applications and ethical considerations in the translation field.

4.3.3 Risks associated with using GenAI tools in translator training

The last set of questions focused on the potential risks associated with using GenAI tools in translator training. These risks were examined in terms of their impact on both translation and translator competence. The results of the analysis show that both sets of variables were measured reliably, with a Cronbach's alpha coefficient of 0.833 for the first group and 0.897 for the second. Additionally, the Kaiser-Meyer-Olkin measure indicated an appropriate level of association between variables in both sets, with a KMO of 0.795 for the first group and 0.826 for the second. The Bartlett's test of sphericity was significant for both sets of variables, with $\chi2(10) = 346.1$ and $p < 0.001$ for the first set concerning dangers for translation products, and $\chi2(10) = 481.2$ and $p < 0.001$ for the second set concerning translator competence. Finally, the exploratory factor analysis revealed that both sets of dangers were unidimensional and did not have any subareas.

As for the values of factor loadings, the results of the exploratory factor analysis are listed below:

Variables (risks for translation)

- decreased translation quality: 0.893
- decreased language quality: 0.840

Table 4.6 Opinions on the extent to which GenAI tools (e.g. ChatGPT) should be used in translator training (by role/profession and age)

		Role/profession (p = 0.073)			Age (p = 0.951)			
		Translator	Translation teacher	Translation student	20–29 (A)	30–39 (B)	40–49 (C)	50+ (D)
limited, e.g. only minimal use for exemplary illustration	n	19	9	5	5	5	12	11
	%	35.2	20.9	9.3	9.4	21.7	32.4	28.9
small, e.g. restricted use in specific training modules or exercises)	n	11	3	22	22	6	2	6
	%	20.4	7.0	40.7	41.5	26.1	5.4	15.8
moderate, e.g. moderate use as a supplementary resource for trainees	n	15	21	21	21	9	16	11
	%	27.8	48.8	38.9	39.6	39.1	43.2	28.9
big, e.g. regular use in various aspects of translator training	n	4	8	5	4	3	6	4
	%	7.4	18.6	9.3	7.5	13.0	16.2	10.5
significant, e.g. extensive use as a vital resource playing a substantial role in training	n	5	2	1	1	0	1	6
	%	9.3	4.7	1.9	1.9	0.0	2.7	15.8

p – probability in Kruskal-Wallis test.

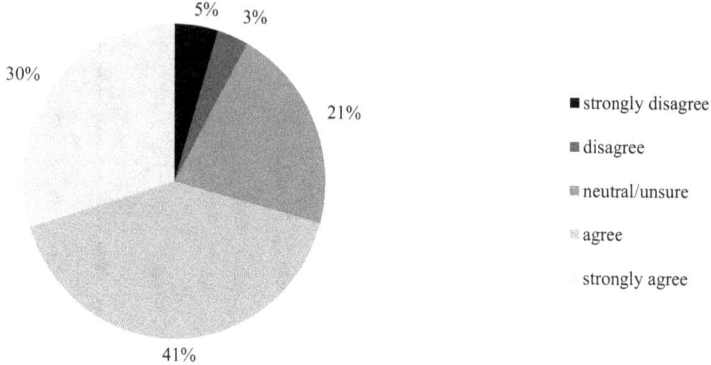

Figure 4.8 Opinions on whether translation educators should be trained in using GenAI for pedagogical purposes (shown in percentage).

- potential mistranslations or misinterpretations: 0.818
- reduced cultural nuances: 0.771
- ethical concerns: 0.584

Variables (risks for translator competence)

- gradual deterioration of language skills: 0.873
- gradual deterioration of translation skills: 0.866
- overreliance on the assistance of the tool: 0.834
- difficulties in critically evaluating translations: 0.832
- reduced creativity and originality in translation: 0.805

The factor loadings clearly indicate the crucial role of the analysed factors in evaluating the risks posed by GenAI to the translation industry. Each factor loading is above 0.5, with many exceeding this threshold by a significant margin. This confirms that the questions chosen to assess the hazards associated with GenAI were well-chosen. For a comprehensive overview of the responses to questions about potential dangers, please see Figure 4.9.

Regarding the product of translation, respondents expressed the greatest concern about reduced cultural nuances (M = 4.14, SD = 0.91, Me = 4) and potential mistranslations or misinterpretations (M = 4.10, SD = 0.83, Me = 4). Three out of four respondents confirmed these

Table 4.7 Opinions on whether translation educators should be trained in using GenAI for pedagogical purposes (by role/profession and age)

		Role/profession (p = 0.002**)			Age (p = 0.131)			
		Translator	Translation teacher	Translation student	20–29 (A)	30–39 (B)	40–49 (C)	50+ (D)
strongly disagree	n	6	0	1	1	0	1	5
	%	11.1	0.0	1.9	1.9	0.0	2.7	13.2
disagree	n	2	0	3	2	1	1	1
	%	3.7	0.0	5.6	3.8	4.3	2.7	2.6
neutral/unsure	n	15	6	11	12	5	6	9
	%	27.8	14.0	20.4	22.6	21.7	16.2	23.7
agree	n	15	16	31	32	9	13	8
	%	27.8	37.2	57.4	60.4	39.1	35.1	21.1
strongly agree	n	16	21	8	6	8	16	15
	%	29.6	48.8	14.8	11.3	34.8	43.2	39.5

p – probability in Kruskal-Wallis test.

98 Attitudes towards AI in translation

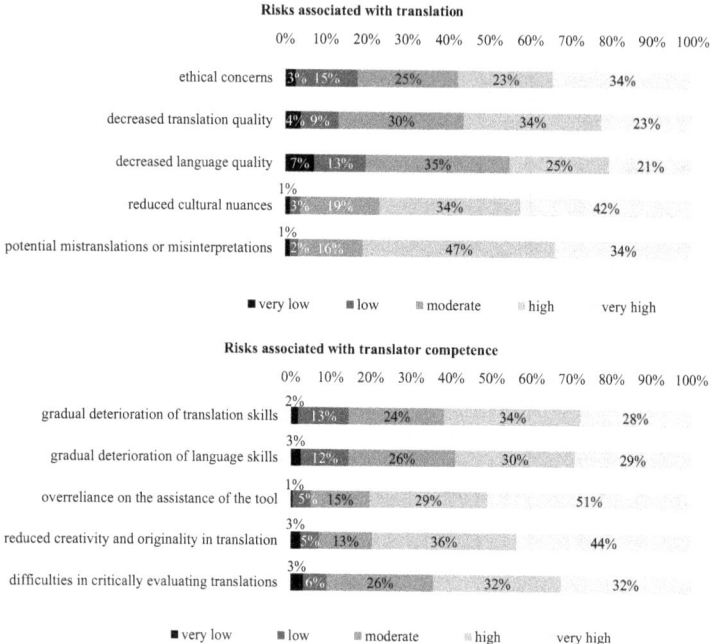

Figure 4.9 A comprehensive overview of the responses to questions about potential dangers.

risks, with less than 5% disagreeing. Decreased language quality was seen as the smallest danger (M = 3.38, SD = 1.16, Me = 3), with slightly less than half of individuals agreeing and every fifth person disagreeing (see Figure 4.9 and Table 4.8). Importantly, exploratory factor analysis showed that the distribution of individual variables was not highly skewed (see Table 4.9).

Respondents in different roles/professions held similar opinions regarding the most serious dangers associated with the translation product (Kruskal-Wallis test p > 0.05). However, two other issues had statistically significant differences (see Table 4.8). Translators perceived a higher risk associated with decreased translation quality compared to translation teachers (p = 0.026) and decreased language quality compared to translation students (p = 0.024). Ethical concerns were more strongly expressed by translation teachers than translation students (p = 0.059).

Age did not significantly differentiate opinions on the dangers of GenAI in relation to translation products. The survey results show that respondents are highly concerned about translator competence, with 60–80% of responses indicating a high or very high level of risk associated with this aspect of translator education (see Figure 4.9). The greatest danger identified is "overreliance on the assistance of the tool" (M = 4.25, SD = 0.92, Me = 5), with half of the responses indicating a "very high" level of concern. This evaluation is consistent across different roles and age groups (p = 0.148), although respondents in their forties express greater concern than those in their twenties (p = 0.059) – see Tables 4.8–4.9. "Reduced creativity and originality in translation" is also seen as a significant danger (M = 4.13, SD = 0.99, Me = 4), with 44% of responses indicating a "very high" level of concern. Translators rate this danger significantly higher than translation students (p = 0.033), and respondents in their twenties rate it significantly higher than those in their forties (p = 0.004).

Age and role/profession significantly differentiate the other three issues concerning translators' competences (see Tables 4.8–4.9). Translation students perceive all three issues as posing less risk compared to professional translators, and also considered both "gradual deterioration of language skills" and "difficulties in critically evaluating translations" as less hazardous than did translation teachers.

Respondents in their forties express significantly more concern about all five issues than those in their twenties, and more concern than individuals over 50 about "gradual deterioration of language skills" and "difficulties in critically evaluating translations". Those in their thirties express more concern than individuals in their forties about "gradual deterioration of translation and language skills" (see Table 4.9 for details).

The statistical correlation between the perceived dangers of GenAI and its importance for translations and the translation market is significant (see Table 4.10). Those who hold a negative view of AI tend to perceive its potential consequences more strongly, while those who see it as beneficial are less afraid of the consequences. The negative correlation is particularly strong when it comes to decreased translation and language quality (with correlation coefficients nearing 0.5). However, even those who perceive GenAI as beneficial still rate decreased translation quality as a significant concern (with rho = -0.134 and p = 0.100).

Table 4.8 Risks associated with the use of GenAI tools in translator training (total and by role/profession)

	Total				Role/profession			
					Translator			
	M	Me	SD	S	M	Me	SD	S
Risks associated with translation								
ethical concerns	3.72	4.00	1.17	-0.42	3.69	4.00	1.23	-0.38
decreased translation quality	3.62	4.00	1.06	-0.48	3.81	4.00	1.20	-0.79
decreased language quality	3.38	3.00	1.16	-0.27	3.65	4.00	1.26	-0.70
reduced cultural nuances	4.14	4.00	0.91	-0.93	4.20	4.00	0.96	-1.23
potential mistranslations or misinter-pretations	4.10	4.00	0.83	-0.97	4.15	4.00	0.88	-1.17
Risks associated with translator competence								
gradual deterioration of translation skills	3.73	4.00	1.06	-0.48	3.96	4.00	1.08	-0.95
gradual deterioration of language skills	3.71	4.00	1.09	-0.45	3.83	4.00	1.19	-0.70
overreliance on the assistance of the tool	4.25	5.00	0.92	-1.10	4.24	5.00	0.99	-1.24
reduced creativity and originality in translation	4.13	4.00	0.99	-1.23	4.26	5.00	1.07	-1.51
difficulties in critically evaluating translations	3.84	4.00	1.05	-0.68	4.07	4.00	1.03	-0.81

* $p < 0.05$, ** $p < 0.01$, *** $p < 0.001$. M – mean, Me – median, SD – standard deviation, S – skewness.

The level of concern surrounding the potential risks of GenAI seems to be somewhat influenced by the variety of translation tools that the respondents use. Upon analysing the outcomes presented in the final column of Table 4.10, it can be concluded that a greater diversity of tools utilised does not necessarily result in increased apprehension regarding translation products ($p > 0.05$). However, there is a stronger correlation with perceiving hazards related to translators'

Translation teacher				Translation student				Kruskal-Wallis test			Post hoc tests
M	Me	SD	S	M	Me	SD	S	H	df	p	
4.02	5.00	1.14	-0.65	3.50	4.00	1.09	-0.40	5.446	2	0.066	TS < TT (p = 0.059)
3.30	3.00	1.12	-0.11	3.67	4.00	0.78	-0.33	6.894	2	0.032*	TT < T (p = 0.026*)
3.07	3.00	1.22	0.11	3.37	3.00	0.94	-0.11	7.148	2	0.028*	TS < T (p = 0.024*)
4.07	4.00	1.03	-0.96	4.13	4.00	0.75	-0.22	0.928	2	0.629	n.a.
3.95	4.00	0.92	-0.85	4.17	4.00	0.69	-0.59	1.597	2	0.450	n.a.
3.72	4.00	1.22	-0.34	3.50	4.00	0.86	-0.46	6.989	2	0.030*	TS < T (p = 0.025*)
3.93	4.00	1.06	-0.49	3.41	3.00	0.96	-0.39	7.821	2	0.020*	TS < TT (p = 0.042*) TS < T (p = 0.059)
4.42	5.00	0.88	-1.39	4.13	4.00	0.87	-0.80	3.821	2	0.148	n.a.
4.21	4.00	1.01	-1.45	3.94	4.00	0.88	-0.93	7.142	2	0.028*	TS < T (p = 0.033*)
3.98	4.00	1.10	-0.96	3.50	4.00	0.97	-0.65	10.585	2	0.005**	TS < T (p = 0.007**) TS < TT (p = 0.040*)

capabilities, although the association's strength is not significant (correlation coefficients range from -0.089 to -0.253 and demonstrate a negative correlation). A wider range of tools utilised is significantly linked, in a statistical sense, to lower levels of concern regarding a "gradual deterioration of translation skills" (rho = -0.253) and "language skills" (rho = -0.173), as well as "reduced creativity and originality in translation" (rho = -0.175).

Attitudes towards AI in translation

Table 4.9 Risks associated with the use of GenAI tools in translator training (total and by age)

	20–29				30–39			
	M	Me	SD	S	M	Me	SD	S
Risks associated with translation								
ethical concerns	3.55	4.00	1.12	-0.46	3.74	4.00	0.96	-0.09
decreased translation quality	3.72	4.00	0.79	-0.40	3.35	3.00	0.78	-0.08
decreased language quality	3.40	3.00	0.97	-0.09	3.09	3.00	0.95	-0.53
reduced cultural nuances	4.11	4.00	0.75	-0.19	4.43	4.00	0.59	-0.45
potential mistranslations or misinterpretations	4.13	4.00	0.68	-0.55	4.17	4.00	0.65	-0.18
Risks associated with translator competence								
gradual deterioration of translation skills	3.55	4.00	0.87	-0.43	3.43	4.00	1.08	-0.05
gradual deterioration of language skills	3.47	4.00	0.97	-0.44	3.52	3.00	1.12	0.05
overreliance on the assistance of the tool	4.17	4.00	0.85	-0.73	4.09	4.00	0.95	-0.88
reduced creativity and originality in translation	3.98	4.00	0.84	-0.96	4.13	4.00	0.92	-1.05
difficulties in critically evaluating translations	3.49	4.00	0.95	-0.60	3.96	4.00	1.02	-1.31

* p < 0.05, ** p < 0.01, *** p < 0.001. M – mean, Me – median, SD – standard deviation, S – skewness.

It is worth noting that respondents who declare that they use GenAI tend to be less fearful of the consequences for both translation products and translators' competence. For each concern, the average rating among users of GenAI is lower than that of users of other tools (see Table 4.11).

40–49				50+				Kruskal-Wallis test			Post hoc tests
M	Me	SD	S	M	Me	SD	S	H	df	p	
4.05	5.00	1.22	-0.69	3.61	4.00	1.26	-0.38	5.279	3	0.152	n.a.
3.73	4.00	1.33	-0.76	3.53	3.50	1.22	-0.30	3.854	3	0.278	n.a.
3.51	3.00	1.39	-0.36	3.42	4.00	1.29	-0.46	2.380	3	0.497	n.a.
4.22	5.00	1.03	-1.26	3.92	4.00	1.10	-0.74	4.311	3	0.230	n.a.
4.16	4.00	0.90	-0.58	3.95	4.00	1.04	-1.27	0.768	3	0.857	n.a.
4.19	5.00	1.10	-1.06	3.71	4.00	1.16	-0.71	12.852	3	0.005 **	A < C (p = 0.007**) B < C (p = 0.025*)
4.27	5.00	1.04	-1.20	3.61	4.00	1.13	-0.57	15.332	3	0.002 **	A < C (p = 0.001**) B < C (p = 0.034*) D < C (p = 0.037*)
4.59	5.00	0.76	-1.93	4.13	4.50	1.07	-1.11	8.739	3	0.033 *	A < C (p = 0.053)
4.51	5.00	0.90	-2.45	3.97	4.00	1.22	-0.99	12.014	3	0.007 **	A < C (p = 0.004**)
4.35	5.00	0.95	-1.19	3.76	4.00	1.13	-0.58	17.819	3	<0.001 ***	A < C (p < 0.001***) D < C (p = 0.063)

The most substantial differences are observed when evaluating "decreased translation quality" – users of TMS rate this danger 0.52 points higher than those who use GenAI (averages of 3.71 vs. 3.19), although the differences are still evident even when compared to users of other tools (averages higher by 0.33–0.37). The assessment of reduced

Table 4.10 Correlation analysis of perceptions regarding GenAI's benefits, market impact, usage versus risk evaluation

		How beneficial do you find generative AI (e.g. ChatGPT) for translation?	What impact might generative AI have on the translation market?	How many AI tools do you use?
ethical concerns	rho	-0.178	-0.159	-0.061
	p	0.029*	0.051	0.453
decreased translation quality	rho	-0.479	-0.381	-0.132
	p	<0.001***	<0.001***	0.107
decreased language quality	rho	-0.459	-0.335	-0.146
	p	<0.001***	<0.001***	0.074
reduced cultural nuances	rho	-0.352	-0.282	-0.120
	p	<0.001***	<0.001***	0.141
potential mistranslations or misinterpretations	rho	-0.343	-0.239	-0.108
	p	<0.001***	0.003**	0.186
gradual deterioration of translation skills	rho	-0.298	-0.327	-0.253
	p	<0.001***	<0.001***	0.002**
gradual deterioration of language skills	rho	-0.217	-0.249	-0.173
	p	0.007**	0.002**	0.034*
overreliance on the assistance of the tool	rho	-0.134	-0.237	-0.089
	p	0.100	0.003**	0.278
reduced creativity and originality in translation	rho	-0.172	-0.331	-0.175
	p	0.035*	<0.001***	0.031*
difficulties in critically evaluating translations	rho	-0.183	-0.213	-0.154
	p	0.024*	0.009**	0.059

Table 4.11 Usage of AI tools and opinions on the potential risks associated with using GenAI tools in translator training (means comparison)

Potential risks	Translation Management Systems, e.g. Trados, Phrase, MemoQ etc.	Machine translation, e.g. DeepL, Microsoft Translator, Google Translate, Amazon Cloud, etc.	Generative AI, e.g. ChatGPT, Google Bard, etc.	Writing assistants and checking tools, e.g. Grammarly, Microsoft Editor etc.
ethical concerns	3,66	3,71	3,58	3,81
decreased translation quality	3,71	3,52	3,19	3,56
decreased language quality	3,42	3,28	3,05	3,26
reduced cultural nuances	4,08	4,16	3,81	4,20
potential mistranslations or misinterpretations	4,12	4,09	3,86	4,10
gradual deterioration of translation skills	3,66	3,63	3,47	3,53
gradual deterioration of language skills	3,59	3,63	3,60	3,63
overreliance on the assistance of the tool	4,22	4,22	4,05	4,33
reduced creativity and originality in translation	4,03	4,09	3,86	4,16
difficulties in critically evaluating translations	3,84	3,81	3,65	3,74

Table 4.12 Hierarchy of risks associated with using GenAI tools in translator training correlated with AI technologies used by respondents

Translation Management Systems, e.g. Trados, Phrase, MemoQ etc.	Machine translation, e.g. DeepL, Microsoft Translator, Google Translate, Amazon Cloud, etc.	Generative AI, e.g. ChatGPT, Google Bard, etc.	Writing assistants and checking tools, e.g. Grammarly, Microsoft Editor etc.
overreliance on the assistance of the tool	overreliance on the assistance of the tool	overreliance on the assistance of the tool	overreliance on the assistance of the tool
potential mistranslations or misinterpretations	reduced cultural nuances	potential mistranslations or misinterpretations	reduced cultural nuances
reduced cultural nuances	potential mistranslations or misinterpretations	reduced creativity and originality in translation	reduced creativity and originality in translation
reduced creativity and originality in translation	reduced creativity and originality in translation	reduced cultural nuances	potential mistranslations or misinterpretations
difficulties in critically evaluating translations	difficulties in critically evaluating translations	difficulties in critically evaluating translations	ethical concerns
decreased translation quality	ethical concerns	gradual deterioration of language skills	difficulties in critically evaluating translations
ethical concerns	gradual deterioration of translation skills	ethical concerns	gradual deterioration of language skills
gradual deterioration of translation skills	gradual deterioration of language skills	gradual deterioration of translation skills	decreased translation quality
gradual deterioration of language skills	decreased translation quality	decreased translation quality	gradual deterioration of translation skills
decreased language quality	decreased language quality	decreased language quality	decreased language quality

cultural nuances also differs quite significantly (M = 3.81 for users of GenAI versus about 4.1 for other tools). Users of GenAI are similarly concerned, compared to others, about "overreliance on the assistance of the tool" (M = 4.05 versus 4.22–4.33 for others). However, like the others, they are least concerned about decreased translation and language quality.

Table 4.12 illustrates the ranked dangers of using GenAI tools in translator training presented in correlation with AI technologies used by respondents.

Although there are some minor variations, the ranking remains consistent across all four groups. It should be highlighted that the majority of respondents declared using tools from at least two groups concurrently, which needs to be taken into account in the analysis of the findings.

4.4 Summary of the findings: challenges and lessons learned

There is a clear trend favouring GenAI integration into translator education, with only a minority of respondents (below 10%) expressing the view that incorporating AI is unnecessary, as illustrated in Figure 4.9 (Section 4.3). In this case, translation teachers exhibit a more pronounced inclination towards integration than translators (see Table 4.8). It indicates a broad support for using GenAI tool in translator training, with the overwhelming majority of respondents (more than 90%) supporting the idea that translation students should receive such training. The use of standard deviation (SD = 1.03) indicates variability in responses, but the relatively high mean and median point towards overall favourable opinions.

The data shows varying levels of GenAI adoption among different age groups and roles, suggesting that technology acceptance and the learning curve associated with GenAI tools could be an important aspect to explore further. Younger translators and students seem more adaptable or open to integrating new technologies, which could imply that newcomers to the translation market are more inclined to embrace GenAI as a regular part of their toolkit. This trend could lead to a generational shift in how translation work is performed and perceived.

The interest in bringing AI to the translation classroom is the strongest among translation teachers who are directly involved in translator education, which suggests that they recognise the potential of embracing technological advancements like GenAI in educational settings. Translators might exhibit more reluctance towards the integration of AI in translator training, compared to the surveyed teachers, for several reasons, reflecting concerns about practical implications, job security and the nature of their future work.

As discussed in Section 3.4, translators may fear that increased reliance on AI and automation could lead to reduced demand for their services and thus threaten their job security. Translators might also worry that an overemphasis on AI in training could lead to a devaluation of these human-centric skills or an overreliance on technology that might not always produce translations of comparable quality or integrity (see Section 2.4 on ethical considerations). This fear is also reflected in the negative correlation between the perceived dangers of GenAI and its importance for translations and the translation market (see Table 4.11) which is particularly strong when it comes to decreased translation and language quality (with correlation coefficients nearing 0.5). Indeed, translators might perceive AI tools as a threat or at least as useful aids but not as replacements for human judgement and expertise. In contrast, translation teachers – focused on a broad range of educational goals – might see AI as a valuable addition to the curriculum that can enhance learning and expose students to cutting-edge technology.

The use of AI in translation can also raise ethical concerns, particularly among translators, including issues related to data privacy, confidentiality and the potential for bias in AI algorithms (see Section 2.4). Translators might be more acutely aware of these issues due to their direct interaction with sensitive or proprietary information, making them more cautious about embracing AI. What is more, the reluctance of translators towards AI in translator training can also be justified with the fact that adapting to new technologies requires time and effort, which might be seen as an additional burden. Translators who are already established in their methods might view the integration of AI as a challenge to their workflow or an unnecessary complication, preferring to stick with familiar tools and techniques. Last but not least, the introduction of AI may understandably pose a challenge to the translators' self-concept, as delineated in Section 3.5, potentially diminishing the esteem in which their expertise is held. Consequently, they may want to avoid placing any value in interactions with AI as it would necessitate a recalibration of their professional identity.

Nonetheless, it should be highlighted that a greater proportion of translators (9%) compared to other groups (2–5%) view the extensive application of AI as an essential tool in training. Translator teachers displayed a notably higher frequency of "moderate" responses here (approximately 50%), with a reduced incidence of "low" feedback (28%). This indicates that there is a discernible variation in perceptions regarding the significance of AI in translation training, with translators – on the one hand – showing more reluctance, but – on the other hand – if they show an inclination towards the importance of AI in training it is clearly stronger than in the remaining groups. In this case, translation teachers exhibit a more balanced perspective, as evidenced by their higher propensity for moderate assessments and a lower tendency towards minimal agreement.

Still, a noticeable reluctance among translators is evident, as further illustrated by additional remarks provided in the final optional open-ended question of the survey. For instance, one of the translators (with former experience in teaching) made the following comment regarding AI introduction in translator training:

[Translator 1]
You should be training students how to use their brains rather than how to use tools. I used to teach translation at postgraduate level. Anyone can use tools. Not everyone can think.

An even more radical viewpoint emerges in another comment (Translator 2 below) where the resistance to AI takes on a more pronounced form, advocating for a complete prohibition of GenAI tools in translator training and academic settings.

[Translator 2]
I think that generative AI tools should be banned in translator training and at the university level because they jeopardise language, culture, etc. The major concern with these tools is that the user takes for granted that everything provided is accurate. That's why the user should carefully consider the outcome to avoid any mistranslations. Another major concern is that using such tools, it will be extremely difficult to train trainers who can afford to deliver a lecture and conduct practical exercises for translation students. In other words, the user will be another machine, only excelling in transforming a text from one language into another. Finally, the choice of whether to use generative AI tools or only have recourse to traditional tools is like whether to train in a manual or automatic car. Training on the second will not enable the user to use the first.

Several concerns addressed by Translator 2 caution against uncritical acceptance of AI assistance, which could potentially lead to the deterioration of language and cultural understanding in translation and the diminishment of translator competence. Apparently, the primary concern expressed in Translator 2's apprehension is the presumption of accuracy in the output of these tools, which could potentially lead to complacency among users. To mitigate the risks mentioned here, a more critical and cautious engagement with AI tools is indeed necessary for upholding the standards of both translation and translator education.

Beyond the debate regarding the incorporation of GenAI into translator training, numerous thoughtful observations were shared in this closing section of the survey, highlighting the diverse perspectives on the general application of GenAI in the field of translation. Within the spectrum of comments revealing attitudes towards AI and its role in translation, some of the remarks expressed doubt and scepticism as for the possible AI contribution in this field, asserting that AI is useless in translation.

[Translator 3]
I am a medical translator. In my field public MT and AI cannot be used due to confidentiality. They can be used only in closed systems of, for example, LSPs.

[Translator 4]
AI is no intelligence at all – it is simply a rip off from existing work. It not only takes future work from translators (evolution is a normal thing) but uses copyrighted material without paying a single cent to the rights owners. This does not only apply to translation but also to design, music, writing, and any creative endeavour. It is a scam.

[Translation student 1]
Current AI is completely useless.

The perspective presented by Translator 4 highlights a contentious issue regarding the sourcing and use of copyrighted material by AI technologies and the potential economic implications for the human workforce. Coupled with Translation student 1's categorical viewpoint, such an approach shows a belief in the insurmountable gap between AI capabilities and the requirements for high-quality translation, emphasising the current technological limitations. However, with the current pace of GPT development and the looming advent of AGI, the validity of these arguments may soon come into question.

The opinions diverge significantly across the professional landscape, capturing an array of perspectives that range from outright rejection to cautious non-engagement. This variance is particularly pronounced as some viewpoints reveal that certain respondents have not engaged with AI technologies, thus reflecting a spectrum of interaction levels with AI in the context of translation.

[Translation teacher 1]
I have not used generative AI for the purpose of translation. I depend on DeepL Translator and corpus dictionaries, such as Glosbe. Generative AI can make things up as far as I understand, and this freedom to create is questionable when dealing with the need to be precise. I am not sure about the quality of generative AI translation so it is hard for me to judge. I have not used generative AI and do not plan to use it, unless DeepL Translator is also generative AI in some sense, then I view it rather positively.

[Translator 5]
I have not yet used Chat GPT (and similar tools) in a translation. In the end, is it not the case that we will always need a person who is able to say that what the machine has produced is nonsense? This is especially so if we conceive of language as an endlessly recombinable system. For example, in my use of DeepL there are occasions on which it has produced risible and/or inaccurate sentences. I often have to translate Polish from earlier centuries in texts with highly specialised vocabularies. Here again, machines produce highly unsatisfactory results.

Some respondents, such as Translator 6, simply do not like AI and express a distinct dislike for using it in translation. Translator 6 finds AI unappealing, stating a personal preference for translating independently. Additionally, concerns were raised about the potential negative impact on the translation industry, positing that AI could lead to its decline.

[Translator 6]
I find AI unappealing since I get a kick out of doing my own text generation. It will also destroy large parts of the translation industry, if this is defined as the translators. For the customer, the

result is likely to be an improvement in average price-for-quality. Like it or not, there's no doubt AI is the future and every new translator needs to know it inside out.

However, this translator also acknowledges that for customers, AI might lead to improvements in the price-quality ratio of translation services. Despite personal reservations, Translator 6 concedes that AI is undeniably the future of the field, emphasising the necessity for new translators to become thoroughly familiar with it.

Some respondents exhibit very positive inclinations towards the use of AI in translation, particularly emphasising the potential benefits when these technologies are integrated thoughtfully into practice and education. Translation Teacher 2 exemplifies this viewpoint, arguing that AI tools, especially GenAI, are indispensable in modern translation.

[Translation teacher 2]
AI tools in general and generative AI in particular are realities that simply cannot be ignored. Used properly and judiciously, they constitute perhaps the most valuable tools translators have ever had at their disposal. They simply must be adequately included as a key component in translator education and thus form an essential element in the repertoire of translator educators, who need detailed knowledge and hand-on experience of how the systems work and where their strengths and weaknesses lie.

Voices such as that of Translation Teacher 2 advocate for the thorough integration of AI as an essential tool in translator training, emphasising that such technologies are among the most valuable resources currently available to translators.

Another noticeable trend identified in the survey is that certain respondents adopt a passive approach towards AI in translation, choosing neither to actively oppose nor to advocate for the technology, but rather to remain unengaged.

[Translation teacher 4]
Paracelsus, a German-Swiss physician and alchemist, once said, "All things are poison, and nothing is without poison; the dosage alone makes it so a thing is not a poison." It can equally apply to the use of AI in translation. To be aware of its drawbacks as well as

to learn how to employ it properly is the challenge for both translation teachers and professionals of the field. However, we can't underestimate its potential.

[Translator 8]
AI and certain poisons have similar effects. Both can help in small doses.

This group recognises the inevitability of AI's integration into their professional sphere and opts for a pragmatic, if passive, acknowledgement of its presence. They seem to advocate for a balanced perspective, suggesting that while AI introduces new challenges, it also offers undeniable efficiencies and capabilities. This approach reflects the belief that, similar to any powerful tool, the effectiveness of its use depends not on its inherent qualities but on how it is handled.

Finally, the last discernible viewpoint from the survey reveals that some respondents display a slightly more reflective stance, accepting the use of AI in translation yet remaining visibly cautious about its implications. This viewpoint acknowledges the potential benefits of AI but is also acutely aware of and recognises the serious risks inherent in its use.

[Translator 7]
Do you remember the scene in the film "Blade Runner" when Deckard applies the Voight-Kampff test to Rachel because Tyrell asks him to? Well, i do remember it and as a translator it comes to my mind every day when I have to edit pretranslated or machine-translated jobs ... Because we translator are becoming mere readers now. So often it's perfect, but most of the material is "false", "artificial", it lacks "flow", the natural way of humans speaking ... For now it's OK, i am still capable of amend it because i have a linguistic background, but my "fear" is that in the near future this strange language will impose and nobody, no Deckard, no test, will detect it and nobody will care at all ... But that will be for everything, nobody will read el Quijote, etc. Thank you very much, great initiative!

[Translation teacher 3]
In general, if used reasonably, AI might facilitate translation. However, it might result in overreliance on AI and, consequently,

decreased translation quality. As a supervisor and a reviewer, I have already seen some diploma theses of students who wanted to facilitate the writing process by writing in Polish or Ukrainian (given the students' native languages) and translating the texts into English, using Google Translate. The results were sometimes embarrassing, for example, as a reviewer, I saw "drowning people" instead of "Utopians", or "Lovecraftovsky" (seemingly a family name, even though it was supposed to be an adjective) in a BA thesis on Lovecraft, and the students had not even taken the trouble to read the results of machine translation and correct such evident errors. Similarly, there are websites whose foreign language versions have been created by translation software, for example, a tourism website translates "kultura kociewska" as "Kittian culture". Thus, I am afraid that overreliance on AI might aggravate such problems and make them more widespread. Of course, students should be taught about translation software, but they should also be taught to approach it with caution, for example, when to use it and when not to use it.

Translator 7 is reflecting on how translators are increasingly becoming validators of machine output rather than creators of translations, which shows a cautious acceptance, tempered by concerns about losing the natural flow of human language. Indeed, the advent of MT has already distorted the translator's role to some extent and the further advancement of AI technologies threatens to push this transformation further. The traditional image of the translator as an active mediator is increasingly giving way to the role of a post-editor or a linguist specialising in substantive and stylistic text correction. As AI takes over more of the routine translation tasks, translators find themselves primarily refining and correcting machine-generated texts, rather than crafting translations from the ground up.

Similarly, Translation Teacher 3 acknowledges the potential for AI to aid in translation but warns against overreliance that could lead to poor quality and misunderstandings. This cautious stance stems from a concern that, as AI becomes more prevalent in translation, the deeper, human aspects of language could be lost, leading to a detachment from traditional literary works and the very essence of human expression. This caution reflects a profound consideration for the long-term implications of AI on linguistic integrity and cultural heritage. Both perspectives underscore a balanced approach, recognising the benefits of AI while advocating for vigilance to maintain quality and authenticity in translation.

The perspectives shared by the respondents provide a rich basis for future considerations and actions to be taken by translation educators. Given the range of opinions, from outright rejection to cautious acceptance, it is clear that GenAI needs to be integrated into translator education in a balanced manner that respects and addresses the varied concerns of professionals in the field. Future efforts could focus on developing guidelines that outline best practices for using GenAI in translator training, ensuring that these tools are used to complement rather than replace human skills. Many respondents express concerns about GenAI's quality and ethical implications, such as privacy issues and the potential for producing culturally insensitive or incorrect translations. Future studies and training programs could aim to establish ethical guidelines and quality assurance protocols that ensure GenAI tools adhere to the high standards expected in professional translation. What is more, students, professional translators and their clients should be educated about state-of-the-art GenAI tools and the level of privacy they offer, which could mitigate potential misunderstandings and debunk some false beliefs.

With strong support among translation teachers for incorporating GenAI into education, there is an opportunity to develop curricula that not only teach how to effectively employ these tools in everyday work but also critically assess their outputs. This includes training on AI's current limitations, fostering skills to evaluate and refine AI-generated translations, as well as monitoring and adapting to AI's progress. This leads to another issue – mitigating the digital divide. The comments provided by the respondents show a discrepancy among translators in terms of their exposure to and comfort with AI tools. It is critical for translation teachers to offer training to those less familiar with GenAI technologies, assuring that those willing to adapt are not left behind as the industry evolves.

Finally, the concerns about GenAI's long-term impacts on the translation profession require a public debate. Given AI's extensive application across virtually all sectors of the economy, its pervasive presence is a concern that must be openly and decisively addressed. Such debates could foster a more constructive dialogue about the future of AI in translation, helping to clarify misconceptions and allowing to address the challenges and concerns seen by professionals. In the authors' view, these debates should finally progress beyond simply recognising the necessity to discuss AI usage and actively engage in addressing specific issues, integrating these concerns into a deliberate approach.

Notes

1 The authors gratefully acknowledge the support of an expert statistician, Professor Justyna Wiktorowicz from the Department of Social and Economic Statistics at the University of Łódź, Poland.
2 Please note that during the survey, the term TMS was used instead of CAT tools for clarity purposes. This is because TMS encompasses a wider range of tools, including regular CAT tools. As the most prominent tools in the market are both TMS and CAT tools at the same time, the Authors opted for a more generalised reference to ensure clarity.

References

Walesiak, Marek, and Eugeniusz Gatnar. 2009. *Statystyczna Analiza Danych z Wykorzystaniem Programu R*. Warszawa: Wydawnictwo Naukowe PWN.

Wiktorowicz, Justyna. 2016. 'Exploratory Factor Analysis in the Measurement of the Competencies of Older People'. *Econometrics. Ekonometria. Advances in Applied Data Analytics*, 4 (54): 48–60.

5 Implications for translator training

5.1 To teach or not to teach?

The integration of AI tools into translator education is increasingly gaining attention in the field of translation studies, especially concerning its role in translator training programs. As AI-driven translation technologies become more sophisticated, the question arises whether AI should be a fundamental component of translator training, or whether its incorporation risks undermining the development of human translation skills. The following section explores the arguments for and against teaching AI in translator training, assessing its applicability and the extent to which it can be used in education, acknowledging its potential effects on the future of the translation profession.

As observed in the findings of the study (Sections 4.3–4.4), translator teachers and professional translators acknowledge the imperative for students to develop independent translation skills, free from reliance on technological assistance. However, the practicality of integrating AI technologies in education is difficult to ignore, given the demands imposed by market realities. The dynamic nature of the language industry presents both challenges and opportunities for professionals in the field. As observed by Shreve (2019), the rapid evolution of job requirements and the continuous emergence of new technologies mean that job descriptions often serve merely as a preliminary guide for understanding employer needs. This fluidity necessitates a curriculum that is not only responsive to current industry standards but also anticipates future trends and technologies.

As observed by Zhu (2023: online), "with its increasing application in all sectors of life, the use of artificial intelligence or machine translation is on its way to becoming mainstream in the translation industry". Considering the prevalence of technology in professional and academic settings, integrating AI tools into education prepares students for future challenges where such tools are commonplace (Hayes, 2023). While addressing concerns about authorship, plagiarism (Barnett, 2023; Longoni et al., 2023) or overreliance is crucial (Amato & Schoettle, 2023), a thoughtful integration of AI can be a pragmatic approach to equip students for the demands of modern reality. Consequently, integrating AI technologies in translator training becomes essential, offering a forward-looking approach that prepares students for the complexities of the translation profession. In doing so, educational institutions can foster a generation of translators who are not only adept at navigating current technologies but are also capable of adapting to and adopting future innovations, ensuring their relevance and competitiveness in the ever-evolving language services industry.

The introduction of AI into the classroom signifies a recognition that learners will inevitably utilise it for various purposes, including mundane tasks such as composing home assignments or completing final projects. Expecting students to refrain from using AI tools for writing or translating may indeed be unrealistic, with arguments in favour of this perspective highlighting benefits such as increased efficiency, improved learning outcomes and better preparation for real-world scenarios. Efficiency stands out as a significant benefit, with AI tools facilitating the writing process and enabling students to focus on content development. Moreover, the use of AI encourages engagement with advanced language suggestions, fostering improved language skills and writing proficiency (Zhang et al., 2023).

Advocates for incorporating AI into translator training highlight its potential to equip future translators with skills necessary for success in a technology-driven market, enhancing productivity and offering new services like post-editing (O'Brien, 2007; Guerberof Arenas, 2013; Guerberof-Arenas & Moorkens, 2023). As observed by Bowles and Kruger (2023: 75), "to be able to fulfil students' expectation of better prospects in the job market, educators will need to ensure students are equipped to use generative AI, rather than insulate them from it". Integrating AI tools into translation education can help future translators remain competitive and responsive to market demands.

However, a heavy reliance on technology in translator training might put academic integrity at risk and potentially compromise the development of essential translation skills, such as bridging cultural gaps in a creative and idiomatic way, which AI has yet to replicate. In addition to concerns about overreliance on AI systems in translator training environments, ethical issues associated with AI – such as job security and the perpetuation of biases – indicate the necessity for a comprehensive training approach that includes ethical considerations alongside technological proficiency (Hayes, 2023). A balanced curriculum that combines AI tool instruction with a strong foundation in linguistic, cultural and ethical knowledge presents a viable solution. Such an approach enables translators to retain the critical human touch necessary for quality translation and still remain deeply aware of the societal impacts of AI systems. This nuanced strategy ensures that the translation profession advances without sacrificing its essential human essence, preparing translators to navigate the complexities of their field effectively.

Translation as a practice is deeply embedded within environmental elements, extending far beyond the mere cognitive process of translating between languages. That is why the current trend in translator education has been towards real-world authentic and experiential learning (Kolb, 1984; González Davies, 2004; Klimowski, 2015; Kiraly, 2016). The approach presented here addresses the challenge of enhancing graduates' employability by ensuring they have genuine experience with the technologies they will encounter in their careers. AI technologies have fundamentally altered not only translation workflows but also the educational environments dedicated to training future translators. As technology continually evolves, translators and interpreters must adapt and develop new skills to remain competitive and proficient in their profession. These changes necessitate a reevaluation of traditional pedagogical approaches to accommodate the evolving landscape.

Educational institutions dedicated to translator training must remain vigilant regarding technological advancements, ensuring students gain firsthand experience with the industry's tools and methodologies. Achieving this requires not only the integration of AI technologies into translation classrooms and other translation environments but also extending beyond courses focused solely on technology. Moreover, students should be encouraged to engage with these technologies to hone their information literacy and evaluate the opportunities and challenges.

However, in today's translator training, the emphasis on technological competence alone is insufficient and should not dominate the educational discourse. Angelone (2023) advocates for a stronger focus on adaptive expertise in translation and translator training to enable optimal performance in today's language industry. The significance of self-development and continuous self-directed learning (Knowles, 1975; Zimmerman et al., 1992) reinforces the notion of translator education as an ongoing process. Prioritising the development of adaptable competencies alongside technological proficiency appears essential for ensuring that future translators are well-prepared to thrive in contemporary translation services. The engagement of translation students in their own learning process facilitates sustained involvement in their professional development.

5.2 What's in it for translation students?

Given the abovementioned demands and expectations within the translation industry, the importance of integrating AI technology into translator training programs has been increasingly recognised. Prior to the advent of artificial intelligence, numerous strategies were proposed to approach translation technologies in the translation curriculum (e.g. Marshman and Bowker, 2012; Kenny & Doherty, 2014; Pym, 2014; Gaspari et al., 2015; Mellinger, 2017, 2018). Approaches to familiarising students with digital resources are not limited to technological tools but include empowering students and equipping them not just with the knowledge of using MT, but also with the skills to critically evaluate and effectively integrate these technologies into their work (Moorkens, 2018), thereby enhancing their translation competencies and marketability.

Similarly, incorporating AI technologies into translator training – apparently a necessity given the industry's increasing reliance on technology – requires a comprehensive approach that balances technical proficiency with ethical and practical considerations. The introduction of AI in translator education cannot be limited to teaching students how to use new tools. Instead, it necessitates a comprehensive curriculum that addresses the ethical, practical and technical aspects of AI in translation. If executed effectively, this approach can potentially offer significant benefits to students, making it a valuable and productive investment of time.

Introducing AI into translator training programs brings advantages, especially in terms of automating tasks (Amato & Schoettle, 2023: 19), language quality and accuracy improvements. AI-powered proofreading and editing tools represent a leap forward in assisting students to refine their translations. These tools go beyond simple grammar checks; they analyse the text for style, clarity and fluency, ensuring that translations not only are grammatically correct but also read naturally in the target language. Additionally, AI can play a crucial role in enhancing consistency across translations. It helps maintain uniformity in terminology and stylistic choices, a critical aspect often challenging for humans to keep track of, especially in large projects (see Section 1.1.4 for more information). This consistency is vital in professional translation settings, such as legal or technical documents, where precise terminology is crucial.

The educational process can benefit greatly from automated translation evaluation tools, offering both teachers and students immediate insights into the quality of translations. AI-based tools can objectively assess translations against a set of criteria, providing detailed feedback that helps pinpoint areas of strength and weakness. This instant feedback mechanism allows students to make immediate adjustments, fostering a more dynamic and responsive learning environment. The ability to instantly see where improvements are needed can accelerate the learning process, making it both efficient and effective. Moreover, using AI-driven analysis of specific language pairs in translator training can open up new learning opportunities thanks to enabling quick identification and clarification of the linguistic challenges of communication in a particular pair of working languages. AI's capability to recognise patterns in errors can direct attention to common pitfalls, enabling targeted practice and instruction. This insight may be invaluable in discussions and practices aimed at developing strategies to overcome specific obstacles, ultimately improving translation accuracy.

As observed by Massey & Ehrensberger-Dow (2017: 307–308),

> students should be encouraged to develop the metacognitive capacity to reflect on the deployment of language technologies, by learning about the capabilities and limitations of the machines

and tools with which they are and will be working. To mitigate the constraints and the physical and cognitive ergonomic risks presented by their TM systems and CAT tools, they should receive early and repeated training in ergonomics and in customising and adapting the technology to meet their own needs – and not the other way around.

The authors highlight the essential role of metacognitive development in translator education, emphasising the need for students to critically engage with the language technologies they utilise (see Section 5.4).

The integration of technology in the translation process necessitates a proactive and informed approach from the educational sector. Translator educators hold the crucial responsibility of designing programs that not only impart technical proficiency to students but also cultivate the personal resources and metacognitive skills essential for a competent use translation technologies. But still, this integration is a necessity. As observed by Bowles and Kruger (2023: 76), technology democratises education by making it accessible outside of universities, so higher education must retain its competitive advantages over self-teaching with technology. What is invaluable here is the human connection that occurs between educators and students and among students themselves when they cooperate, but also the "formation of potentially lifelong professional, and social, networks for students" and the "guarantee to employers and others of knowledge, skills, and abilities that a degree confers" (ibid.).

By fostering an environment that encourages exploration, customisation and reflection, translator educators can prepare aspiring translators to use and control technology effectively, thereby enhancing their productivity and job satisfaction. Prioritising ergonomic training (Ehrensberger-Dow & Massey, 2014; Massey & Ehrensberger-Dow, 2017) and metacognitive skills (Haro-Soler, 2018, 2019; Haro-Soler & Kiraly, 2019; Pietrzak, 2022) within translation programs can cultivate a new generation of translators who are not only technologically savvy but also critically engaged with their work environment. This approach will ensure that young translators are well-equipped to meet the challenges of the digital age, marking a significant step forward in the evolution of the translation profession.

Implications for translator training

5.3 Suggested ways of introducing AI-assisted translation practice

Given all the efficiency gains offered by AI technologies and the demands of the modern translation market, embracing the newest technologies in translation education seems obligatory in order to prepare students comprehensively and ethically for contemporary translation practice. Below, the authors present some exemplary ways in which AI technologies can be integrated into translation courses. The section aims to provide training practices, such as practical exercises and training practices that incorporate AI tools for pedagogical purposes.

5.3.1 Exercises in AI-assisted translation

Trainee translators can develop their technical skills and digital resilience by engaging in the use of AI for translation to critically analyse the output and perform post-editing tasks. Such exercises are intended to enhance students' technical proficiency, post-editing skills, critical thinking and the awareness of AI limitations.

Exercise description:

AI-assisted translation exercise

1. **Translation assignment**: students use AI technology for initial translation.
2. **Evaluation**: students assess the quality with a focus on specific interest area.
3. **Follow-up:** post-editing, refining and improving.
4. **Discussion**: exploring AI tool challenges.

In this exemplary exercise, students can be provided with a source text for translation and asked to evaluate an AI-generated target text. To provide a more focused approach, the analysis can be guided to concentrate on specific areas of interest relevant to the given training objectives. For instance, key areas of focus for this training exercise could include the following aspects that may require attention in such a training practice:

124 *Implications for translator training*

- identifying inaccuracies;
- assessing cultural appropriateness;
- evaluating consistency in terminology and style;
- identifying nuances and subtleties lost in translation;
- analysing the effectiveness of tone and register for the target audience;
- checking for completeness, ensuring no content has been omitted;
- examining grammar, punctuation and spelling for language accuracy;
- reviewing the translation for readability and natural flow in the target language;
- detecting calques, direct translations and overreliance on source language structures;
- evaluating the handling of specific terms (e.g. colloquialisms, gender-specific nouns, idiomatic expressions, technical jargon, regional dialects, euphemisms, cultural references etc.).

Next, students can be asked to meticulously refine the translations through deliberate, thoughtful, manual intervention. Following this, a class discussion can be conducted to explore the challenges associated with using the chosen AI tool.

5.3.2 AI tools for terminology management

AI tools offer sophisticated solutions for terminology management – the process of systematically collecting, managing and updating terms stored in a specialised database to maintain quality and consistency, especially in specialised translation. AI-powered terminology management can automate the identification, extraction and application of terms across texts. Exploring the functionalities, benefits and limitations of these tools can help trainee translators evaluate their effectiveness, choose the most suitable tools and apply them to translation projects.

Exercise description:

AI-assisted terminology management

1 **Terminology extraction**: students use AI-powered tools to extract terminology from a given text (or batch of texts) on a given specialised topic.

2 **Termbase**: students use AI-powered tools to organise extracted terms into a termbase, which can later be used standalone or through CAT tools.
3 **Consistency check**: students apply the termbase to identify and correct terminological inconsistencies in the target text.
4 **Discussion**: exploring challenges related to AI-powered tools.

In this scenario, students use selected AI tools to identify and extract key terms and phrases in the given set of documents on a specialised topic. This process involves setting up the tool (if it is a standalone program), choosing the right parameters for extraction (such as frequency of occurrence, relevance to the topic, etc.), designing a proper prompt for the AI and running the extraction process. Next, students use AI tools to categorise and organise those terms into a termbase, adding relevant information such as definitions, context, source language, target language equivalents, and any notes on usage, similarly to the process of creating termbases for CAT tools. In fact, a secondary goal of the activity can be to create a termbase that could be integrated with CAT tools or used as a standalone reference. Finally, when students use the termbase and AI-powered tool within a new or existing translation project to identify and correct any terminological inconsistencies, they compare the project's terminology with that of the termbase and make necessary adjustments.

Key areas of focus for this training exercise include several aspects that will enable students to better understand AI's role in enhancing terminological consistency and overall translation quality:

- evaluating the precision with which AI tools identify and extract key terms and phrases relevant to the specialised topic;
- ensuring that the extracted terms cover all necessary aspects of the subject area;
- analysing how effectively students can set up the AI tools, including designing effective AI prompts;
- assessing how well the terms are categorised and organised within the termbase, including the adequacy of definitions, context, source and target language equivalents and notes on usage (if applicable);
- evaluating the ease with which the created termbase can be integrated with CAT tools or used as a standalone reference, as well as how this integration impacts the translation workflow;

- assessing the effectiveness of using the termbase and AI-powered tools for the identification and correction of terminological inconsistencies within translation projects;
- evaluating how well the AI tools and termbase handle specialised terms (e.g. technical jargon, industry-specific language and any other terms that require precise understanding and usage).

Once all the steps have been completed, it is worth asking students to reflect on the activity and share their experiences, challenges faced (such as inaccuracies in term extraction, difficulties in termbase management, etc.) and the overall effectiveness of AI tools in maintaining terminological consistency, so that they can improve their collective understanding of the process.

5.3.3 AI-assisted quality assessment

The exercise outlined below is designed to develop practical skills in terms of AI-assisted quality assessment. It is intended to familiarise them with processes such as AI-assisted review, analysis and revision, which can not only help sharpen their skills but also show them a critical perspective on the role of technology in shaping the future of translation.

Exercise description:

AI-assisted quality assessment

1 **Translation**: students translate a short text in groups without the aid of AI tools initially, relying solely on their own expertise.
2 **AI-assisted review**: each group inputs their translated text into the AI tool to receive feedback on quality, consistency, error detection and suggested corrections.
3 **Analysis**: students analyse the AI-generated feedback and compare it with their own translations; they identify errors, inconsistencies and issues not evident to human translators at first glance.
4 **Revision**: students revise their translations based on the AI feedback, focusing on critical evaluation of AI suggestions.
5 **Follow-up**: each group presents their original and revised translations, discussing how AI-assisted quality assessment influenced their revisions and what they learned from the process.

6 **Discussion:** students engage in the discussion on the benefits and limitations of AI-assisted quality assessment.

In this scenario, students learn about AI-assisted quality assessment, exploring the usability, functionality and significance of these tools in the translation industry. The teacher introduces a specific AI tool (e.g., an online platform that offers machine translation and quality assessment features) that will be used for the exercise, detailing its features and how it can help in identifying and correcting translation errors.

The first task for students is group work on a short text which is to be translated without the aid of AI. Then they are to run AI-based evaluation of the quality of their translations, receiving feedback on quality, consistency, error detection and suggested corrections. Finally, they are to analyse the AI-generated feedback, comparing it with their own translations. A discussion on the identified errors or inconsistencies follows, highlighting issues that may not be evident to human translators initially. The discussion can focus on some of the key aspects of AI-assisted quality assessment in translation:

- automatic detection of errors (e.g. grammatical, syntactic, spelling);
- consistency checks across the translated document (e.g. uniformity of terms and style);
- contextual analysis for semantic accuracy (e.g. intended meaning, cultural nuances);
- areas that may require human intervention during the stage of post-editing;
- identification of areas for student improvement.

In this training exercise, students gain hands-on experience with AI-assisted quality assessment tools in translation, learning to critically evaluate AI-generated feedback to improve translation quality and understanding strengths and limitations of AI in this area.

5.3.4 AI-generated feedback

In this scenario, students are introduced to AI-generated translation feedback and shown how it can be obtained and used in their own translation workflow. Trainee translators can use AI-generated translation feedback not only to enhance the translation workflow by gaining real-time insights, suggestions and corrections, but also to develop critical evaluation skills with respect to AI-generated suggestions and learn to make conscious decisions when improving translation quality.

Exercise description:

AI-generated feedback

1. **Translation**: students translate a short text without the aid of AI tools initially, relying solely on their own expertise.
2. **AI-generated feedback**: students use AI tool to generate feedback for their translation based on pre-set conditions.
3. **Revision**: students use the feedback to revise their translations, focusing on improving the identified weak points.
4. **Critical evaluation**: students review the AI-generated feedback, discussing its relevance and accuracy in the context of their translations.
5. **Reflections**: students share their experiences working with AI-generated feedback.

To enhance effectiveness, the feedback can be customised to align with the specific needs of students, ensuring it is delivered in a format that best supports their learning. This customisation might consider various factors including the extent of the students' specialised background knowledge, the desired level of detail in the feedback, the degree of descriptiveness or the focus on providing only a concise list of errors alongside recommended revisions.

In addition to customisation, students can use an AI tool to generate targeted feedback for their translation based on pre-defined criteria that align with the intended purpose or the areas of focus designated by the teacher. It is important to establish clear criteria that correspond with educational goals and address specific areas for improvement. Here are some example criteria that teachers might establish for AI-assisted feedback practice, focusing on specific aspects of the target text being revised by the AI:

- **grammar** – check for grammatical correctness and review sentence structure for clarity;
- **style, tone and register** – match the original style and tone, adjust the formality as necessary, change the register and adjust it to a particular type of audience, etc.;

- **lexical resource** – check for appropriateness of word choice and use of specialised terms relevant to the subject matter, suggest synonyms to enrich language and evaluate vocabulary for diversity, lexical appropriateness, idiomaticity etc.;
- **accuracy** – check for fidelity to the source text, verify the accuracy of facts and figures, monitor for any instances of ambiguity, unclear expressions, mistranslations, omissions, additions, etc.;
- **cultural appropriateness** – identify any cultural inaccuracies and adjust the text to the specific target audience that may be unfamiliar with the source language culture;
- **coherence and cohesion** – analyse the logical flow, structure, use of appropriate cohesive devices etc.;
- ***skopos* alignment** – verify if the translation serves its intended purpose, e.g. informative, persuasive, descriptive etc.;
- **consistency** – check for consistent use of terminology and style throughout the translation, e.g. maintain a formal tone, use legal terms throughout, medical language aimed at non-expert patients etc.;
- **further AI assistance** – provide suggestions for areas that require improvement; suggest self-study ideas, explain the rules of a particular grammatical issue or punctuation rules in the target language.

Setting such criteria can help AI provide precise, constructive and individualised feedback, focused on the student's specific needs, thereby – ideally – facilitating improvement in translation skills.

5.3.5 Ethical code of conduct in AI use

The use of GenAI tools can be seen as a breach of confidentiality, especially when the bias around the legality of some of the GPTs' training data is taken into account (see Plant et al., 2022; Ray, 2023; Wang et al., 2024). Therefore, trainee translators must understand the ethical code of conduct for using AI in translation, as they will often work with textual data owned by others and subject to confidentiality agreements.

The purpose of this exercise is to develop deep understanding of the ethical challenges and considerations in students when applying GenAI to their translation projects. They can learn to apply ethical standards to real-world scenarios, enhancing their decision-making skills in professional settings.

130 *Implications for translator training*

Exercise description:

Ethical code of conduct in AI use

1 **Theoretical introduction**: the teacher starts with addressing key topics such as data privacy, intellectual property, bias in AI tools and the accountability of AI-assisted outputs.
2 **Case study analysis**: students work in groups on different case studies which present ethical dilemmas in AI-assisted translation.
3 **Developing standards**: students examine the ethical issues presented in their case studies, discussing potential solutions and developing guidelines.
4 **Presentation and discussion**: students present developed guidelines to the class, discuss ethical dilemmas and analyse the consequences of different actions.

In this training exercise, students can be provided with ethical guidelines from translation companies or AI organisations to review in order to better understand the standards for ethical conduct in AI-assisted translation. It is important to try and develop guidelines that reflect industry standards, but are also tailored to the specific ethical challenges encountered in the respective case studies. When students work on case studies that present specific ethical dilemmas, the focus areas may encompass examples such as:

- confidentiality breaches (sensitive documents where disclosure could have severe consequences);
- intellectual property (proper permissions and attributions for copyrighted material);
- cultural sensitivity (cultural appropriation and respecting source cultures in translations);
- AI bias (addressing biases in AI tools that may affect interpretation);
- accuracy (precise translation versus adaptation).

In the final stage of the exercise, groups present their case studies, ethical dilemmas and proposed guidelines to the rest of their peers. Each presentation can be followed by a discussion session, where other students have the opportunity to question, challenge and suggest improvements to the proposed solutions.

5.4 Fostering personal resources in translator training

The integration of AI technologies in translator training goes beyond technical skills acquisition (see Sections 3.2 and 5.1). It necessitates nurturing students' personal resources to ensure they not only become proficient in using AI tools but also develop the metacognitive capacity required to stay resilient in the dynamic field of translation. Fostering their metacognitive capabilities can contribute to empowering translation students to meet the demands of the digital age with confidence and adaptability. The following training practices aim at promoting a proactive approach to skill development, emphasising the cultivation of key personal resources. It suggests strategies for translators to enhance their metacognitive translator competence which is invaluable in complementing AI tools. By suggesting such an approach, the authors hope to contribute to transforming apprehension into empowerment, enabling future translators to control AI advancements for their professional growth and success in the field.

5.4.1 Self-reflection: what am I missing?

Metacognitive translator competence can be fostered through the implementation of reflective methodologies within translator training programs. Reflection is identified as a fundamental mechanism driving learner transformation (Miller, 1996; Mezirow, 1981), as demonstrated in practices such as experiential learning (Schön, 1983; Mezirow, 1990, 2003). Reflective approaches can be used in translator training, for instance through situated learning (Gouadec, 2007; Kelly, 2005; Kiraly, 2000; Risku, 2010; Way, 2008, 2019), which emerges as a pedagogical strategy that emphasises the importance of authentic contexts for the training of translators and interpreters. This approach posits that learning is most effective when trainees engage in roles, collaborate and integrate within real-life or highly simulated work environments (González-Davies & Enriquez Raído, 2019: 1). Such settings, whether within or beyond the translation classroom, are designed to mimic the complexities and dynamics of professional translation and interpreting tasks, thereby fostering a context-dependent acquisition of skills and competencies.

In the context of translator training, reflective approaches necessitate encouraging students to engage in both reflection and self-reflection (Kußmaul, 1995; Hansen, 2006; Norberg, 2014; Pietrzak,

2019), aiming to enhance their individual autonomy and facilitate self-discovery. Through such pedagogical strategies, learners are prompted to critically evaluate their own experiences, beliefs and practices within the translation process. This critical engagement not only fosters a deeper understanding of their own cognitive and metacognitive processes, but also promotes the development of a more self-directed approach to learning and professional growth (Knowles, 1975). By prioritising reflection and subsequent actions, wherein learners utilise their resources to convert self-reflection into strategic actions (Klimkowski, 2019), translator training programs can equip students with the tools necessary for continuous improvement and adaptation in the dynamic field of AI-assisted translation.

A reflective training practice can, for instance, involve comparing students' translations with those generated by AI to determine the differences between the two outputs. The primary objective of this exercise is, however, not to evaluate the translations' quality and effectiveness. Instead, the focus is on reflection and identifying what elements may be lacking. In this training practice, students are not going to assess the superiority of the AI-enhanced translation, but the focus here is on determining what they may be missing and why.

In this exercise, students are encouraged to engage in self-reflection by asking questions such as in the following example.

Self-reflective gap analysis

Exercise description:

1 **Identifying gaps**

 What am I missing?
 What *particular* aspects have I been overlooking?
 What *specific* concepts am I not fully understanding or applying effectively?

2 **Recognising weaknesses**

 What are my shortcomings?
 Where *precisely* do my weaknesses lie?
 What are the *specific* limitations in my skills, behaviours or thought processes?

3 Focusing on improvements

What do I need to improve?
What *specific* areas require my attention?
What *actionable* steps can I take to enhance these areas?

Having identified gaps, students move on to a deeper analysis of personal weaknesses or limitations in their skills, behaviours or thought processes. It is an introspective look at the root causes of these gaps and how they manifest in students' performance.

The insights gained by students through this training practice may lead to a greater appreciation for the importance of self-development and the enhancement of personal weaknesses. These weaknesses may not necessarily stem only from human limitations but also from the need to develop certain linguistic skills, practise grammar, improve style, fill gaps in cultural knowledge or address transfer-related challenges.

The aim of this reflective exercise is not to assert the superiority of any external technological aid, but rather to comprehend the additional skills that students must develop to function effectively without such support when necessary. Identifying what is missing allows students to understand the specific areas they need to work on, effectively creating a plan for future learning activities. This clarity in what needs to be improved helps translation students to organise their learning process. As a result, having such a plan can make students feel more confident because they know what steps they need to take to develop their translator competence.

This approach not only fosters a more focused and reflective learning experience but also aligns with the principles of lifelong learning. In this context, lifelong learning entails not only staying abreast of the latest developments in translation technologies, but also ongoing self-development to strengthen areas of weakness. This type of practice emphasises the importance of continuous learning, where students must recognise their shortcomings to create opportunities for improvement. It is crucial for students to first identify their deficiencies and understand the exact areas requiring improvement tailored to their unique needs. Recognising these gaps highlights the need for enhancement precisely in the areas where improvement is necessary, encouraging students to conceptualise the particular skills and abilities they need to develop.

5.4.2 Self-efficacy: building digital resilience

In order to support translation students' confidence in their capacity to master translator competence in AI-driven world, translator educators may consider creating environments that support the growth of self-efficacy. Self-efficacy, as outlined by Bandura (1989, 1997), is central to human agency, since "among the mechanisms of agency, none is more central or pervasive than people's beliefs about their capabilities to exercise control over their level of functioning and environmental demands" (Bandura, 1989: 1206). Structured learning experiences, such as collaborative projects (see Kiraly, 2000; González Davies, 2004, 2021), are recognised for boosting self-efficacy by offering chances for interaction, step-by-step skill advancement and joined construction of students' metacognitive capacity (Hadwin et al., 2018).

In the context of translator training and the integration of AI technologies, developing self-efficacy seems essential for students to proficiently use technological aids and adapt to the continuous changes in the field of translation.

This can be achieved through structured learning experiences that offer students various interactions with AI technologies in controlled, yet challenging settings. Educational strategies to build self-efficacy may include providing opportunities for hands-on experience with AI, progressively increasing task complexity and offering feedback that reinforces students' confidence in their capabilities.

An example of a training practice which offers such opportunities is a simulated translation project aiming to enhance self-efficacy and supportive collaboration.

Exercise description:

Resilience-focused simulated translation practice

1 **Team formation**: small groups for collaboration to foster human-led translation.
2 **Adaptive text assignment**: start simple, increase complexity, encouraging critical evaluation over AI-dependency.
3 **Critical AI evaluation**: hands-on experience, promoting a critical approach to their outputs, encouraging discernment and selective utilisation.

4 **Resilience feedback provision**: a constructive and confidence-building discussion of areas for human oversight in the translation task.
5 **Peer review**: a session to share approaches and foster collaboration where teams discuss their decisions and regulation over AI tool.
6 **Reflection and self-reflection**: consideration of balancing AI use with human creativity, identifying areas of human control.

In this exercise, students are divided into small teams and given a real-world text to translate using AI translation tools. Initially, the texts are relatively simple, allowing students to gain familiarity with the AI technology in a low-pressure environment. As the exercise progresses, the complexity of the texts increases, challenging students to apply more sophisticated translation strategies and to critically evaluate the AI's output.

Throughout the project, teachers provide constructive feedback, highlighting both strengths and areas for improvement. This feedback is tailored to reinforce students' confidence in their abilities and to encourage a reflective approach to their work. Additionally, peer review sessions are incorporated, where teams present their translations and discuss the decision-making process behind their work. These sessions not only provide further opportunities for feedback but also promote collaboration and the sharing of insights among students, thereby fostering a sense of a supportive learning community.

Primarily, such a training practice highlights the enduring importance and strength of human intellect and collaboration in the translation process. Its aim is to underscore the importance of resilience in retaining translation capabilities rather than relinquishing them to machines. Working together may be uplifting and serve as a reminder that while AI tools are valuable aids, the essence of translation remains a distinctly human endeavour and technological advancements do not diminish the significance of human expertise and resilience in the field of translation.

5.4.3 *Self-concept: reducing technological anxiety*

This section outlines a potential training practice intended to enhance self-concept while alleviating technological anxieties that stem from integrating AI into translation and translator training. It aims to

136 *Implications for translator training*

engage both translation students and translator educators, recognising the importance of a collaborative approach in facing the challenges presented by AI technologies in translation. Involving both groups is aimed at fostering an environment where concerns can be addressed openly, skills can be developed confidently and the transition to incorporating AI tools can be managed effectively. This ensures a better integration into the educational context of translation, underscoring the role of mentorship and personal interaction in addressing the evolving professional demands of translation (see Felten & Lambert, 2020; Bowles & Kruger, 2023).

Based on the intricate nature of the translator's self-concept (see Section 3.6), an exercise for fostering this aspect of translation students' metacognitive development can be based on a reflective practice designed to deepen their understanding of their professional identity, competencies and the dynamic interplay between their self-concept and translation practices, especially in the context of AI-assisted translations and hybrid workflows.

Exercise description:

The translator's self-reflection journal

1 **Materials preparation:** journal or digital document for recording reflection.
2 **Tasks and prompts:** a series of prompts based on theoretical concepts and practical challenges in translation.
3 **Journal setup**: each student sets up a personal journal dedicated to reflecting on their self-concept as translators.
4 **Reflection prompts**: teacher's prompts that guide their reflections, covering e.g. personal strengths and areas for development, experiences with AI-assisted translation tools, including feelings, challenges and insights.

Reflections entered in the journal do not need to be long and detailed; such entries do not require extensive elaboration as they are only intended to induce students to more readily engage in reflection on their tasks, roles and responsibilities in translation practice. The teacher's prompts may serve to boost the process and guide them in exploring how their knowledge and experiences shape their translation practices, additionally identifying implications for future learning strategies. Such prompts can for instance be as follows:

- How do your skills and knowledge influence this practice?
- How does your experience affect your performance?
- How do you use your past experiences?
- What are your main challenges?
- What lessons have you learned from these challenges?
- How does this task shape your approach?
- What actions will you take to move forward?

This training practice can be followed by group discussions or peer feedback sessions where students share insights from their journals. Collectively, they can observe how their knowledge and experience affect their translation practices and plan ahead for future learning strategies. Constructive feedback and joined exploration of shared experiences can be encouraged to foster a community of practice, enhancing social and constructivist learning.

Assessment criteria are not required for this exercise, as its primary goal is to stimulate engagement with reflection on practical challenges. The emphasis should not be on evaluating the quality or depth of these reflective entries, but rather on their insightfulness and the level of engagement they demonstrate. Therefore, what can be assessed or verified here is merely the presence of the reflective entries, to ensure that students have indeed engaged in the activity. The insightfulness of a reflection cannot be quantified by any specific criteria; its significance stems from the act of reflection itself.

Such a metacognitive activity requires translation students to engage in self-reflection, self-monitoring and self-regulation, which can potentially lead to greater adaptability. It can enhance students' capacity to link personal experiences with translation challenges and wider industry trends, improving their ability to articulate their needs and professional identity. At the very least, it may simplify the process for students to establish personal objectives for honing certain translation skills, formulate strategies for enhancement and create personalised plans for their own professional growth.

References

Amato, Luanne M., and Christine Schoettle. 2023. 'Using Artificial Intelligence Ethically and Responsibly: Best Practices in Higher Education'. In *Creative AI Tools and Ethical Implications in Teaching and Learning*, edited by Jared Keengwe, 19–31. IGI Global. https://doi.org/10.4018/979-8-3693-0205-7.ch002.

Angelone, Erik. 2023. 'Weaving Adaptive Expertise into Translator Training'. In *The Human Translator in the 2020s*, edited by Gary Massey, Elisa Huertas Barros, and David Katan, 60–73. Routledge.

Bandura, Albert. 1989. 'Human Agency in Social Cognitive Theory'. *American Psychologist* 44 (9): 1175–84. https://doi.org/10.1037/0003-066X.44.9.1175.

———. 1997. 'Exercise of Personal and Collective Efficacy in Changing Societies'. In *Self-Efficacy in Changing Societies*, edited by Albert Bandura, 1–45. Cambridge: Cambridge University Press.

Barnett, Sofia. 2023. 'ChatGPT Is Making Universities Rethink Plagiarism'. *Wired*, 30 January 2023. www.wired.com/story/chatgpt-college-university-plagiarism/.

Bowles, Devin C., and Jessica Sloan Kruger. 2023. 'Generating Employable, Intelligent Graduates in a World with Generative AI: Thoughts for Educators'. *Pedagogy in Health Promotion* 9 (2): 75–77. https://doi.org/10.1177/23733799231175171.

Ehrensberger-Dow, Maureen, and Gary Massey. 2014. 'Cognitive Ergonomic Issues in Professional Translation'. In *The Development of Translation Competence: Theories and Methodologies from Psycholinguistics and Cognitive Science*, edited by John W. Schwieter and Aline Ferreira, 58–86. Cambridge: Cambridge Scholars Publishing.

Felten, Peter, and Leo M. Lambert. 2020. *Relationship-Rich Education*. Johns Hopkins University Press. https://doi.org/10.1353/book.78561.

Gaspari, Federico, Hala Almaghout, and Stephen Doherty. 2015. 'A Survey of Machine Translation Competences: Insights for Translation Technology Educators and Practitioners'. *Perspectives* 23 (3): 333–58.

Gonzalez-Davies, Maria. 2004. *Multiple Voices in the Translation Classroom*. Btl.54. John Benjamins. https://benjamins.com/catalog/btl.54.

———. 2021. 'Student Agency in Translator Training: Setting a Framework for Good Practices'. *Research in Language* 19 (2): 117–33. https://doi.org/10.18778/1731-7533.19.2.02.

Gonzalez-Davies, Maria, and Vanessa Enríquez Raído, eds. 2019. *Situated Learning in Translator and Interpreter Training: Bridging Research and Good Practice*. London: Routledge. https://doi.org/10.4324/9780203732304.

Gouadec, Daniel. 2007. *Translation as a Profession*. Amsterdam/Philadelphia: John Benjamins. www.jbe-platform.com/content/books/9789027292513.

Guerberof Arenas, Ana. 2013. 'What Do Professional Translators Think about Post-Editing?' *Journal of Specialised Translation*, 19: 75–95.

Guerberof-Arenas, Ana, and Joss Moorkens. 2023. 'Ethics and Machine Translation: The End User Perspective'. In *Towards Responsible Machine Translation: Ethical and Legal Considerations in Machine Translation*, edited by Helena Moniz and Carla Parra Escartín, 113–33. Springer Verlag.

Hadwin, Allyson, Sanna Järvelä, and Mariel Miller. 2018. 'Self-Regulation, Co-Regulation, and Shared Regulation in Collaborative Learning Environments'. In *Handbook of Self-Regulation of Learning and Performance*, 2nd Ed, edited by Dale Schunk and Jeffrey A. Greene, 83–106. Educational Psychology Handbook Series. New York: Routledge. https://doi.org/10.4324/9781315697048-6.

Hansen, Gyde. 2006. 'Retrospection Methods in Translator Training and Translation Research'. *Journal of Specialised Translation* 5 (1): 2–41.

Haro-Soler, María. 2018. 'Self-Confidence and Its Role in Translator Training: The Students' Perspective'. In *Innovation and Expansion in Translation Process Research*, edited by Isabel Lacruz and Riitta Jääskeläinen, 131–60. Amsterdam/Philadelphia: John Benjamins. https://doi.org/10.1075/ata.xviii.

———. 2019. 'Vicarious Learning in the Translation Classroom: How Can It Influence Students' Self-Efficacy Beliefs?' *English Studies at NBU* 5 (1): 92–113. https://doi.org/10.33919/esnbu.19.1.5.

Haro-Soler, Maria del Mar, and Don Kiraly. 2019. 'Exploring Self-Efficacy Beliefs in Symbiotic Collaboration with Students: An Action Research Project'. *Interpreter and Translator Trainer* 13 (3): 255–70. https://doi.org/10.1080/1750399X.2019.1656405.

Hayes, Catherine. 2023. 'Hyperbole or Hypothetical? Ethics for AI in the Future of Applied Pedagogy'. In *Creative Artificial Intelligence Tools and Ethical Implications in Teaching*, edited by Jared Keengwe. Pennsylvania, PA: IGI Global. http://sure.sunderland.ac.uk/id/eprint/16259/.

Kelly, Dorothy. 2005. *A Handbook for Translator Trainers*. London: Routledge. www.routledge.com/A-Handbook-for-Translator-Trainers/Kelly/p/book/9781900650816.

Kenny, Dorothy, and Stephen Doherty. 2014. 'Statistical Machine Translation in the Translation Curriculum: Overcoming Obstacles and Empowering Translators'. *Interpreter and Translator Trainer* 8 (2): 276–94.

Kiraly, Don. 2000. *A Social Constructivist Approach to Translator Education: Empowerment from Theory to Practice*. Manchester, UK.

———. 2016. 'Authentic Project Work and Pedagogical Epistemologies: A Question of Competing or Complementary Worldviews?' In *Towards Authentic Experiential Learning in Translator Education*, edited by Don Kiraly and Gary Massey, 53–66. Mainz: Mainz University Press.

Klimkowski, Konrad. 2015. *Towards a Shared Curriculum in Translator and Interpreter Education*. Wrocław: Wydawnictwo Wyższej Szkoły Filologicznej.

———. 2019. 'Assessment as a Communicative Activity in the Translation Classroom'. *Intralinea, Special Issue*. www.intralinea.org/print/article_specials/2428

Knowles, Malcolm S. 1975. *Self-Directed Learning: A Guide for Learners and Teachers*. New York: Association Press.

Kolb, David A. 1984. *Experiential Learning: Experience as the Source of Learning and Development*. Vol. 1. Englewood Cliffs, NJ: Prentice-Hall.

Kußmaul, Paul. 1995. *Training the Translator*. Amsterdam: John Benjamins. https://doi.org/10.1075/btl.10.

Longoni, Chiara, Stephanie Tully, and Azim Shariff. 2023. 'Plagiarizing AI-Generated Content Is Seen as Less Unethical and More Permissible', June. https://doi.org/10.31234/osf.io/na3wb.

Marshman, Elizabeth, and Lynne Bowker. 2012. 'Translation Technologies as Seen through the Eyes of the Educators and Students and Educators'. In *Global Trends in Translator and Interpreter Training*, edited by Séverine Hubscher-Davidson and Michal Borodo, 69–95. London: Continuum.

Massey, Gary, and Maureen Ehrensberger-Dow. 2017. 'Machine Learning: Implications for Translator Education', *Lebende Sprachen*, 62 (2): 300–312. https://doi.org/10.1515/les-2017-0021.

Mellinger, Christopher. 2017. 'Translators and Machine Translation: Knowledge and Skills Gaps in Translator Pedagogy'. *Interpreter and Translator Trainer* 11 (4): 280–93. https://doi.org/10.1080/1750399X.2017.1359760.

———. 2018. 'Problem-Based Learning in Computer-Assisted Translation Pedagogy'. *HERMES*, 57: 195–208.

Mezirow, Jack. 1981. 'A Critical Theory of Adult Learning and Education'. *Adult Education* 32. https://doi.org/10.1177/074171368103200101.

———. 1990. 'How Critical Reflection Triggers Transformative Learning'. In *Fostering Critical Reflection in Adulthood: A Guide to Transformative and Emancipatory Education*, 1–20. San Francisco, CA: Jossey-Bass.

———. 2003. 'Transformative Learning as Discourse'. *Journal of Transformative Learning* 1 (1): 58–63.

Miller, John. 1996. *The Holistic Curriculum*. Toronto: OISE Press.

Moorkens, Joss. 2018. 'What to Expect from Neural Machine Translation: A Practical In-Class Translation Evaluation Exercise'. *Interpreter and Translator Trainer* 12 (4): 375–87.

Norberg, Ulf. 2014. 'Fostering Self-Reflection in Translation Students: The Value of Guided Commentaries'. *Translation and Interpreting Studies* 9 (1): 150–64.

O'Brien, Sharon. 2007. 'An Empirical Investigation of Temporal and Technical Post-Editing Effort'. *Translation and Interpreting Studies* 2 (1): 83–136.

Pietrzak, Paulina. 2019. 'Scaffolding Student Self-Reflection in Translator Training'. *Translation and Interpreting Studies* 14 (3): 416–36. https://doi.org/10.1075/tis.18029.pie.

———. 2022. *Metacognitive Translator Training. Focus on Personal Resources*. London: Palgrave.

Plant, Richard, Valerio Giuffrida, and Dimitra Gkatzia. 2022. 'You Are What You Write: Preserving Privacy in the Era of Large Language Models'. *arXiv*. https://doi.org/10.48550/arXiv.2204.09391.

Pym, Anthony. 2014. *Exploring Translation Theories*. 2nd edition. London: Routledge.
Ray, Partha Pratim. 2023. 'ChatGPT: A Comprehensive Review on Background, Applications, Key Challenges, Bias, Ethics, Limitations and Future Scope'. *Internet of Things and Cyber-Physical Systems* 3 (January): 121–54. https://doi.org/10.1016/j.iotcps.2023.04.003.
Risku, Hanna. 2010. 'A Cognitive Scientific View on Technical a Cognitive Scientific View on Technical: Do Embodiment and Situatedness Really Make a Difference?' *Target. International Journal of Translation Studies* 22 (1): 94–111. https://doi.org/10.1075/target.22.1.06ris.
Schön, Donald A. 1983. *The Reflective Practitioner: How Professionals Think in Action*. New York: Basic Books.
Shreve, Gregory. 2019. 'Professional Translator Development from an Expertise Perspective'. In *The Bloomsbury Companion to Language Industry Studies*, edited by Erik Angelone, Maureen Ehrensberger-Dow, and Gary Massey, 153–78. London: Bloomsbury.
Wang, Boxin, Weixin Chen, Hengzhi Pei, Chulin Xie, Mintong Kang, Chenhui Zhang, Chejian Xu, et al. 2024. 'DecodingTrust: A Comprehensive Assessment of Trustworthiness in GPT Models'. *arXiv*. https://doi.org/10.48550/arXiv.2306.11698.
Way, Catherine. 2008. 'Systematic Assessment of Translator Competence: In Search of Achilles' Heel'. In *Translator and Interpreter Training: Issues, Methods and Debates*, edited by John Kearns, 88–103. London: Continuum. www.torrossa.com/gs/resourceProxy?an=5215967&publisher=FZ0661#page=105.
———. 2019. 'Fostering Translator Competence: The Importance of Effective Feedback and Motivation for Translator Trainees'. Intralinea. www.intralinea.org/specials/article/2430.
Zhang, Bo, Jun Zhu, and Hang Su. 2023. 'Toward the Third Generation Artificial Intelligence'. *Science China Information Sciences* 66 (2): 121101. https://doi.org/10.1007/s11432-021-3449-x.
Zhu, Minghai. 2023. 'Sustainability of Translator Training in Higher Education'. *PLOS One* 18 (5). https://doi.org/10.1371/journal.pone.0283522.
Zimmerman, Barry J., Albert Bandura, and Manuel Martinez-Pons. 1992. 'Self-Motivation for Academic Attainment: The Role of Self-Efficacy Beliefs and Personal Goal Setting'. *American Educational Research Journal* 29 (3): 663–76. https://doi.org/10.3102/00028312029003663.

6 Final reflections

The integration of AI into translation education presents a complex yet essential challenge, necessitating a balance between maintaining academic rigour and ensuring students' preparedness for the market. On the one hand, translator educators – whether in academia or other educational settings – uphold standards that discourage shortcuts and reliance on tools that may foster dependency, hindering long-term skill development, but on the other hand, the demands of the translation market prioritise efficiency. Therefore, ensuring that students are adequately prepared for this environment requires them to be familiar with relevant tools.

The findings of the study reveal a cautious inclination towards incorporating AI into the translation classroom, presenting a notable dilemma among professional and academic communities, reflecting both the potential risks and undeniable benefits associated with AI tools in translation training. The concern that AI tools might encourage laziness or impede students' skill development must be balanced against the undeniable need for graduates to be proficient with technologies that boost productivity in the professional translation field. Therefore, it seems imperative for educational institutions to carefully balance traditional methodologies with the implementation of AI technology as a complementary tool, rather than a substitute for foundational learning.

The book advocates for a proactive approach in translator training that integrates AI technologies while respecting the unique human translator expertise. It emphasises that technological skills can complement, rather than overshadow, other educational priorities, such as the enhancement of personal resources and metacognitive skills which actively engage translation students in their learning process, thereby fostering sustained engagement and continuous professional development. When thoughtfully implemented, this balanced integration can mitigate the risk of dependency on AI and foster an environment that enhances students' digital resilience, thereby preparing them for the complex challenges they will encounter in their professional careers.

Such an approach can in fact not only help to maintain academic integrity by embracing technological changes as opportunities for efficiency and growth, but also ensures that translation students are versatile and adept at using new tools, making them competitive in the dynamic translation market. Encouraging responsible educational practices that align with the demands of continuous learning and fostering metacognitive capacities can help translator educators equip future translators with the digital resilience essential for thriving in the digitised, AI-driven world. Currently on the brink technological transformation, both the profession and education communities have the opportunity not merely to react to change but to proactively shape it, ensuring that all members of the translation community remain indispensable in an evolving global marketplace.

Appendix

Attitudes toward AI in translation: an academic exploration

This anonymous survey aims to gather insights into how translators, translator teachers and students approach the question of using generative AI tools (e.g. ChatGPT) in translation industry.

Your responses will contribute to understanding the current trends and challenges faced by translators and translator teachers in approaching AI tools in translation workflows. Please answer the following questions honestly.

1. Please select the option that best describes your current role or profession:
   - translator
   - translation teacher
   - translation student
2. Age:
   - 20–29
   - 30–39
   - 40–49
   - 50+
3. Please specify what AI-powered tools you use when you translate:
   - Translation Management Systems, e.g. Trados, Phrase, MemoQ etc.
   - machine translation, e.g. DeepL, Microsoft Translator, Google Translate, Amazon Cloud, etc.
   - generative AI, e.g. ChatGPT, Google Bard, etc.
   - writing assistants and checking tools, e.g. Grammarly, Microsoft Editor etc.
   - none of the above

4 How beneficial do you find generative AI (e.g. ChatGPT) for translation?
  - extremely beneficial
  - somewhat beneficial
  - neutral/unsure
  - not very beneficial
  - not beneficial at all
5 What impact might generative AI have on the translation market?
  - strongly negative (e.g. leading to job losses and decreased translation quality)
  - negative (e.g. reducing the demand for human translators)
  - neutral (e.g. both positive and negative, with a balance between automation and human expertise)
  - positive (e.g. improved efficiency, reduced costs and increased translation quality)
  - strongly positive (e.g. highly positive impact revolutionising the translation industry)
6 Do you agree that generative AI tools like ChatGPT should be integrated into translator training programs?
  - strongly agree
  - agree
  - neutral/unsure
  - disagree
  - strongly disagree
7 If integrated, to what extent should generative AI tools (e.g. ChatGPT) be used in translator training?
  - limited (e.g. only minimal use for exemplary illustration)
  - small (e.g. restricted use in specific training modules or exercises)
  - moderate (e.g. moderate use as a supplementary resource for trainees)
  - big (e.g. regular use in various aspects of translator training)
  - significant (e.g. extensive use as a vital resource playing a substantial role in training)
8 Do you agree that translation educators should be trained in using generative AI for teaching?
  - strongly agree
  - agree
  - neutral/unsure
  - disagree
  - strongly disagree

9. Please rate the danger of using generative AI tools in translator training (in terms of the translation product; scale: very low – low – moderate – high – very high):
   - ethical concerns
   - decreased translation quality
   - decreased language quality
   - reduced cultural nuances
   - potential mistranslations or misinterpretations
10. Please rate the danger of using generative AI tools in translator training (in terms of translator competence; scale: very low – low – moderate – high – very high):
    - gradual deterioration of translation skills
    - gradual deterioration of language skills
    - overreliance on the assistance of the tool
    - reduced creativity and originality in translations
    - difficulties in critically evaluating translations
11. If you have any additional comments or insights, please share them below and contribute to the ongoing discussion in the field.

Index

Note: Page locators in **bold** and *italics* represents tables and figures, respectively.

adaptable competencies, development of 120
adaptive neural machine translation 32, 35
adaptive text assignment 134
AI-assisted language service provision, ethical considerations in 43–6
AI-assisted language specialists 53
anxiety: archaic 61; automation 61–2; technology-induced 60–4
Artificial General Intelligence (AGI) 19, 20; comparison with ANI and ASI **22**
artificial intelligence (AI) technologies 1–2, 20; adoption of 45–6; advancements in 35; algorithms 14; application in translation 43; challenges introduced by 41; findings on the use in translation 82–91; integration into translation education 142; large language model (LLM) 13; Narrow AI 19; Phrase Language AI 12; risk of dependency on 143; significance of 30; stages of development of 4, 18–24
Artificial Narrow Intelligence (ANI) 19, 20; comparison with AGI and ASI **22**
artificial neural networks 16
Artificial Super Intelligence (ASI) 19, 20–1; comparison with ANI and AGI **22**
augmented reality (AR) 31
augmented translation: concept of 3, 31; rise of 53; technological components of 32–3
augmented translator 34
augmenting human intellect, concept of 31, 35
automated content enrichment (ACE) 32–3
Automated Language Processing Systems (ALPS) 11
automated translation systems 30
automation, concept of 62

Bartlett's test of sphericity 94
breach of confidentiality 129
business practices 60, 68

chatbots, AI-powered 14
ChatGPT 20, 37, *88*, 144–5
chi-square test of independence 79, 81

148 *Index*

clumsy automation, concept of 62
computational linguistics 8–9, 16
computer-assisted translation (CAT) tools 2, 6, 10–13, 15, 17, 38; advancements in 12; concept of 13; ideas behind creation and use of 12; technological evolution 11
computer-assisted web interview (CAWI) methodology 4, 78–9
context-based & retention systems 19
copyright infringement, issue of 44
corpus-based frameworks 11
corpus dictionaries 111
cosmic AI 20
Cramer's V coefficient 79
critical AI evaluation 134
Cronbach's alpha coefficient 94
cryptography, application of 7
cultural appropriateness 34, 39, 124, 129
cultural congruence 53
cultural consultant 53
cybersecurity 19

data privacy 43, 108, 130
data protection regulations 44
decision-making 21, 24, 129
deep learning 10, 15–17, 32
DeepL Translator 9, 14, 111
deskilling, implications of 45
digital age 30, 42, 122, 131
digital divide 115
digital footprint 44
digital resilience 3, 5, 55, 60–4, 62–4, 66, 123, 134, 143

editing 53; AI-powered 121
editorial oversight 52
ethical code, of conduct in AI use 129–30
ethical safeguard 53
Eurolang Optimiser 11
exercises, in AI-assisted translation 123–4
Expert AI Systems 19

facial recognition 20
feedback, AI-generated 127–9
file-processing filters 11
freelance translators 2, 69
fully automated high-quality translation (FAHQT) 8

gender-neutral language 12
generative AI (GenAI) 1, 6, 15, 16–17, 39, 56; capabilities in creative translation 58; capabilities of 38; ChatGPT 144–5; correlation analysis of perceptions regarding **104**; danger of using 146; incorporation in translator education 4–5, 78; integration into translation processes 2; long-term impacts on the translation profession 115; pre-editing for 57; quality and ethical implications 115; quality of the output 57; relation with neural machine translation (NMT) 16; risks posed by **96**, **102**; tools 45; translation 33–4, 36–7
Generative AI Iterative Translation (GAIT) 38–9
generative pre-trained transformers (GPTs) 16
globalisation 30
glossaries 36
God-like AI 20
Google Translate 9, 10
Grammarly 14

High-Level Expert Group on Artificial Intelligence (AI HLEG) 44
human-AI interaction translation workflows 30
human augmentation 31, 34
human cognition 16, 42
human intelligence 19–21, 24, 43; externalisation of 43
human-level AI 20, 23
human-machine collaboration 36
human skill and expertise, devaluation of 42

Index 149

human translation 8, 19, 36, 58, 117
human translators 4, 19, 30, 36;
 AI-assisted language specialists
 51; and AI technologies 1, 4, 55;
 from anxiety to digital resilience
 60–4; development of machine
 aids for 8; future translator
 expertise 53–5; job losses for 42;
 metacognitive capacity of 4; new
 roles and status of 51–3; operating
 within hybrid translation
 workflows 52; personal resources
 and metacognitive capacity
 64–6; professional autonomy 60;
 psychological capital of 4, 54;
 self-concept in AI interactions
 66–8; technical competencies
 of 54; technical skills for hybrid
 workflows 55–60; working as MT
 post-editors 54
hybrid translation workflows 3,
 35–9, 53; adoption of 68; concept
 of 36; rise of 53; technical skills
 for 55–60

information and communication
 technologies 43
information exchange 30
information literacy 120
information theory 7
intellectual property 45, 130
interlingual 'mechanical'
 dictionary 7
internet searches 20

job requirements, evolution of 117
job satisfaction 40, 122

Kaiser-Meyer-Olkin measure 94
Kaiser's criterion 79
knowledge-based systems 19
knowledge management 32
Kruskal-Wallis test 79, 81, 92, *93*

labour market 45
language checking tools 3
language generation modules 3
language technologies 121–2

large language model (LLM) 13, 33,
 37–8
lexical resource 129
lifelong learning, principles of 133
lights-out project management 32,
 35
linguistic proficiency 54
linguistic skills 18, 54, 68, 118,
 133
LLM-client software 39

machine efficiency 18
machine-generated translations,
 quality of 52
machine intelligence 16, 35
machine learning 15, 30, 56, 114;
 AI's application of 40; algorithms
 36
machine translation (MT) 16, 33,
 42–3, 54, 82, 117–18; advantages
 of 36; AI-based 3; ALPAC report
 (1966) 8, 11, 13; Becher's idea of
 7; development of 7; efficiency
 of 35; global interest in 8; goal of
 8; hybrid system 10; integration
 of translation memory with 32;
 MIT conference on 7; neural
 machine translation (NMT) 10;
 problems related with 8; quality
 of output 9; rule-based MT
 (RBMT) 9–10; statistical machine
 translation (SMT) 9–10; as tool
 for translation 6–10
Machine Translation Post-Editing
 (MTPE) practices 39
management of AI tools
 52
Massachusetts Institute of
 Technology (MIT) 7
MemoQ 17
metacognitive capacity 2–4, 63–5,
 68, 121, 131, 134
metacognitive skills 3, 5, 65, 68,
 122, 142
metacognitive translator competence
 65, 131
Microsoft Editor 14
multilingual communication 18

Narrow AI *see* Artificial Narrow Intelligence (ANI)
narrow domain system 19
natural language processing (NLP) 3, 15, 33
neural machine translation (NMT) 10, 17, 32, 55, 57; relationship with GenAI 16

OpenAI 37

peer review 135
personal computers (PCs) 11
Phrase Language AI 12
post-generative AI 21
post hoc tests 81
pre-generative AI 21
problem-solving 21
professional development 42, 55, 68, 78, 120, 143
professional ethics 45
proofreading 53; AI-powered 121
psychological capital 3–4, 54–5, 64–5
psycho-physiological skills 54

quality assessment, AI-assisted 126–7
quality assurance 52; protocols 35

reasoning AI systems 19
recurrent neural networks (RNNs) 10
relationship maps 79, 81, *86*
research on attitudes, towards AI in translation: challenges and lessons learned 107–16; data analysis 81–107; demographic structure of the sample **82**; findings of 107–16; limitations of the study on 79–81; research design 78–9
resilience capability, concept of 64
resilience feedback provision 135
retranslation 53
rule-based MT (RBMT) 9
rule-based systems 16, 18–19

safeguarding client data, importance of 44
SDL Trados 17
self-aware systems 19
self-development, significance of 120
self-directed learning 66, 120
skill development 60, 131, 142
skopos alignment 129
sophisticated terminology management systems 35
Spearman rho coefficient 79
SPSS statistics software 4
statistical machine translation (SMT) 9–10
Statistical Package for the Social Sciences (SPSS) 78
strong AI *see* Artificial General Intelligence (AGI)
SYSTRAN 10

team formation 134
technical skills 54; for hybrid workflows 55–60
technological innovations 42
technology-driven market 118
technology liaison 53
terminology management 11, 32–3; AI tools for 124–6
Transcendent AI 20
transformer architectures 17, 33
translation: AI-powered 59, 82, **84–5**, 123–30; anxiety related to the use of technological tools in 61; cognitive and ergonomic research 61; conventional methodologies of 52; ergonomics of 60; of natural languages 7; reasonable and ethical use of AI-assisted 53
translation competence 54–5, 58, 67
translation education 35; integration of AI into 4–5, 78, 117, 142; perspectives on GenAI integration in 91–4; role of metacognitive development in 122
translation industry 30, 40, 42, 61; market segmentation within 51

Index   151

translation management systems (TMS) 3, 6, 13–14, 39–40, 82
translation memory (TM) systems 3, 11, 32, 36; software 55
translation practice, AI-assisted 59, 82, **84–5**, 123–30; AI tools for terminology management 124–6; ethical code of conduct in 129–30; exercises in 123–4; feedback 127–9; quality assessment 126–7
translation profession, evolution of 122
translation services, professionalism of 43
translation students 120–2
Translation Support System (TSS) 11
translation technology 1, 24; current state of 17–18; development of 6; significance of AI in 30, 117
translation tools: computer-assisted translation (CAT) tools 10–13; generative artificial intelligence in translation 16–17; history and evolution of 6–17; machine translation (MT) 6–10; technological evolution 11; translation management systems (TMS) 13–14; writing assistants and checking tools 14–16
translation trainees 1, 3–4, 46, 78
translation training: in AI tools 53; attitudes toward AI in 144–6; benefits associated with AI tools in 142; cognitive-psychological approaches in 54; implementation of reflective methodologies within 131; psycho-physiological disposition in 54; significance of AI in 109
translator-AI interactions 3, 24, 30–46; augmented translation 30–5; ethical considerations in 43–6; hybrid workflows in translation 35–9; impact of technology on translator profession 39–43
translator competence 4, 55, 63, 65, 67, 69, 94, 99, 110, 131, 133–4
translator educators 1, 3–4, 35, 78, 82, 112, 122, 134, 136, 142–3
translator profession, impact of technology on 39–43
translator training 2, 55, 61; fostering personal resources in 131–7; professional training programs 53; re-evaluation of 53; risks associated with using GenAI tools in 94–107; self-efficacy 134–5; self-reflection 131–3
t-test for correlation 79, 81

ubiquitous computing 31
universal language 7
user interface paradigms 31

virtual assistants 14
virtual identity in usage 54
virtual reality (VR) 31
Voight-Kampff test 113

Weak AI 20
word-for-word translations 7
writing assistants and checking tools 6, 14–16
writing proficiency 118

Z test for proportion 79, 81

For Product Safety Concerns and Information please contact our EU
representative GPSR@taylorandfrancis.com
Taylor & Francis Verlag GmbH, Kaufingerstraße 24, 80331 München, Germany

www.ingramcontent.com/pod-product-compliance
Lightning Source LLC
Chambersburg PA
CBHW051749230426
43670CB00012B/2210